PRIYANKA SINHA JHA

FOLK TALES FROM BOLLYWOOD

ADVENTURES IN TINSELTOWN

Om Books International

First published in 2023 by

Om Books International

Corporate & Editorial Office
A-12, Sector 64, Noida 201 301
Uttar Pradesh, India
Phone: +91 120 477 4100
Email: editorial@ombooks.com
Website: www.ombooksinternational.com

Sales Office
107, Ansari Road, Darya Ganj,
New Delhi 110 002, India
Phone: +91 11 4000 9000
Email: sales@ombooks.com
Website: www.ombooks.com

ISBN: 978-93-94547-04-9

Printed in India

10 9 8 7 6 5 4 3 2 1

For all the wildly curious Bollywood lovers who have posed to me the mischievous question, 'Is it true...?'

Contents

Arty Smarty

MIRZYA IMAN'S EXISTENTIAL GANGSTER FILM, *SHRAPNEL*, OPENS TO HIGH PRAISE AT CANNES, announced the headlines. Mirzya was ecstatic, over the moon. A dream come true – the rousing reception given to his film at the world's biggest film festival. *Dad would have been so proud*, he thought to himself. Mirzya's father had lived and died a junior-level government servant. But, all throughout his life, he had nursed secret dreams of wielding a film director's baton someday. Unfortunately, the dream remained just that – a dream sacrificed at the altar of *rozi-roti*, Mirzya's father had funded his son's education and even his early short films with the savings from his modest salary. Now at forty-five, it finally appeared as though Mirzya had the world at his feet. Or so his deceased father would have thought.

Mirzya preened for the cameras on the dais at the Palais des Festivals on Cannes' famous Croisette. Flanking him on either side were the debutant leads of his film, Zyan Mehta, the young son of yesteryears Bollywood star Meenakshi Mehta, and Sonalika Sengupta, the daughter of Bengali arthouse thespian Shubho Sengupta. With the modest budget of the film, Mirzya's homegrown style of film-making – personal, with an artistic finesse – demanded that the actors put their complete faith in him. Fortunately, with these two greenhorns, fresh out of acting and drama school, it had been easy. Mirzya's reputation as an auteur had preceded him. The two newbies had been thrilled to be debuting with the widely acclaimed director's film even though it was a low-budget art film, and they had worked for virtually peanuts.

Mirzya, however, did try to compensate for the shortcomings of his budget by whipping up some delicious exotic food in his very own kitchen. Legend had it that it was his culinary magic more than his cinematic talent that had enabled him to rope in the Hollywood star Robert Mason in one of his productions. His genius was not just that he cooked well. He would also regale his unit with food trivia attached to each morsel like, "This strain of pilaf (as he chose to pronounce pulao) originated in Persia and then travelled to India through spice traders." Or "Did you know that many dishes like this Jamaican calaloo and this Mauritian dhol puri originated in Bihar?" The flourish with which Mirzya served his delectable delicacies and accompanying facts was a performance worth watching and one which had found numerous admirers.

Over time his film unit had spun such a lore around Mirzya's cooking that a chance to sample Mirzya's fragrant yakhni pilaf and his chelo kebabs were considered adequate trade-off for the low remuneration that people received for working in his films. And then, there was of course that lure of rubbing shoulders with international celebrities, given that Mirzya Iman was a favourite at practically every big international film festival worth talking about. The frequent-flyer miles he had accumulated attending these festivals were enough to get him free flights to all coveted destinations around the world.

Apart from food and film festivals, politics was another favourite subject with Mirzya. The conversations at home throughout Mirzya's childhood alternated between films and politics. After all, his father was a government servant with his ear always to the ground about political developments in the country and over the world.

Not surprisingly then, Mirzya's films were deeply rooted in political realities. Noteworthy among his oeuvre were *Aatma Haran*, about a girl from a backward caste who struggles within the power structure of the Indian bureaucracy, and *Bali*, the spiritual journey of a terrorist. Both films had gathered such high praise that you'd imagine an endless line of suitors from the film industry, but nothing of the sort had happened for Mirzya as yet.

Bollywood trade pundits had declared that Mirzya's films were 'suitable only for a select audience', an industry euphemism for films that have respectable content but low box-office potential. "*Jo dikhta hai woh bikta hai.* Your films are hardly seen outside of film festivals abroad and a few select theatres in metro cities..." Mirzya's dyed-in-the-wool Bollywood film-distributer friend Dipesh Jain would often tell him.

Top film stars, who occasionally professed their love for his work on suitable occasions, ran scared when it came to actually working with him.

"Arrey tera subject bahut risky hai, bhai!"

"At this stage, my managers feel I should stick to the tried-and-tested romance."

"You remember the last time I tried to experiment? I was booed at in cinema halls." These were some of the responses Mirzya often received from his starry friends.

The truth was that Mirzya's films lacked most trappings considered essential for feeding the escapist fantasies of mass Indian audience – no item numbers, no song sequences and, the worst of all, no shoot in exotic locations. And of course, the modest pay cheque could have been a factor too, although every actor denied it vehemently.

Some time back, Mirzya and Ayaaz Khan, the reigning God of the marquee, had connected and spent a few boozy nights talking about the films of Fellini, Charles Chaplin and Satyajit Ray.

One night, over many pegs of the finest scotch, after a passionate discussion about the films of the Coen brothers, Ayaaz had finally confessed to Mirzya that he had been flirting with the idea of working with Mirzya for some time. By the time the booze was running out and dawn was peeping in, Ayaaz declared with gusto, "Let's do a film together, buddy!"

They had even agreed upon a subject – a film based on the true story of a forest officer fighting to save the jungles from unscrupulous politicians and industrialists. And in his enthusiasm, Ayaaz had promptly called Aakash Bakshi, the CEO of a prominent studio to get him on board.

This had obviously made Mirzya a very happy man.

However, when Mirzya sent him the script soon after, there was an inexplicable silence from Ayaaz's side. After a few days, Mirzya called, only to be told by Ayaaz's assistant that the star had left for Bulgaria for three months to shoot for his next film. Eventually, after several messages and repeated emails, Mirzya was informed that Ayaaz's schedule was packed for the next three years with back-to-back projects.

Mirzya had been disappointed and hurt but eventually reconciled himself to operating at the margins of stardom. However, this time with rave reviews of *Shrapnel*, at Cannes, Mirzya was hoping for wider attention on his home turf. And indeed, his phone had been flooded with messages and some rather open propositions of working together.

Alas, much to his surprise when he scanned the newspapers at the airport on his arrival, there were no major mentions in the entertainment section. Mirzya's Cannes success had already become a small footnote. Most of the entertainment section was devoted to the blockbuster *Chutzpah*, a meaningless-comedy starring Bollywood star Manoj Rishi, and the actioner *Patriot* starring Ankur Srivatsa.

The bloody bilge they dish out! Mirzya thought bitterly to himself. *And yet the studio bosses are fawning all over them, ready to throw hundreds of crores their way while giving me the run-around for a couple of measly crores.*

Pawan, Mirzya's production manager-cum-right-hand man, welcomed him outside the airport. After the congratulations and pleasantries they headed straight to Mirzya's ramshackle barracks-like office in Aaram Nagar, Versova. On the way, Mirzya asked for an update on the outcome of Pawan's meetings over the last fortnight with distributors for *Shrapnel*.

The look on Pawan's face suggested that all was not well. Pawan did not want to disappoint his boss, but the news was grim. "All of them say it's too slow for the normal cinema-loving junta," Pawan mumbled. Nobody, absolutely nobody, except small single-screen distributors had shown an interest. And that too it was because of the couple of gunfights and intimate scenes in the film which would probably bring in the audience in the morning shows.

Mirzya shuddered at the fate of his much-loved, feted work of art about the homegrown weapons industry. "What! My film is no better than a porn film in India!" he yelled, in frustration.

Pawan cleared his throat. "No sir. Porn films make a lot of money. They are certainly lucrative…"

He caught Mirzya's angry expression and checked himself quickly. "But I would not go so far as to advise you to start making them."

There was a brief silence as the two men reached Mirzya's small, spartan office. Inside, they flopped onto divans that lined the walls and gazed at the floor tiles with such purpose that one would imagine the answer was hidden somewhere underneath their polished surface. Finally, Mirzya broke the silence.

"Damn! What do I do now? I'll have to settle for an OTT release for *Shrapnel*. But, those corporate guys are super-smart, they'll promise to package and market it well, but I'll be lucky if I recover even half of the production budget of the film. I need to announce a new project quickly and get in some money to pay off the creditors I had tapped for making the film. If I don't do that, I am finished … Ruined," Mirzya shouted dramatically, pacing the length of his office.

"Absolutely! Let's announce and start making the next project. But it should have a subject that is not too … uh … arty," said Pawan cautiously.

"Pray tell me, who will finance a non-arty film by me?"

"Don't worry, sir. Your creative genius still has many takers," Pawan replied without skipping a beat. He knew how to modify his unflattering thoughts into encouraging words that Mirzya needed to hear right now.

Pawan had worked with Mirzya for five years now and genuinely admired the man. After a lot of hustling in small jobs as a production assistant, Pawan had been hired as a production manager by Mirzya. He wanted to turn producer one day, and had realized that Mirzya was possibly the only man who would give him a break in that capacity. Provided Mirzya didn't self-sabotage his brilliant career beforehand.

But things looked bleak for arty film-makers in general and Mirzya in particular. All of Mirzya's earlier partners-in-crime who believed in avant-garde cinema had run out of steam. Amit Varma and Shashilal Zaveri who had funded several independent film-makers were no longer sitting on HNI funds to invest in films. And Mirzya's public spat with Ayaaz after his cold rejection had not helped. Ayaaz had ensured that Aakash Bakshi rejected all his proposals, even the small-budget short-film series!

Mirzya's phone rang just then. Mirzya motioned to Pawan to answer it. He was in no mood for entertaining a random salesman calling to check if he wanted a loan.

"Yes. Sir is in a meeting. I will check with him and get back. But he should be able to," Pawan trilled over the phone after exchanging a few words with the caller.

He cut the line and said, "Sir, you have to attend a party in the evening. Former cabinet minister Purohit Pandey is the host – his office is e-mailing a formal invite, so please don't skip."

Purohit Pandey was a former minister and politico from UP who had shot to fame and prominence in the last decade and was rumoured to have amassed a fortune way beyond his income.

"What does that dolt want from me?"

"Oh, the usual, he wants to surround himself with glamorous intellectuals and bask in their reflected glory," replied Pawan.

Pawan quickly checked his e-mail on his phone. The invite was already in his inbox.

"I was right. The invite says it's just a gathering of friends from different walks of life to cross-pollinate ideas and foster a culture of creativity. Just your kind of party, sir," he said cheekily.

Mirzya's indefatigable spirit had hit rock bottom. He had expected a grand reception of sorts from the crème de la crème of Mumbai, instead he was being invited to a political buffoon's desperate attempt at self-aggrandizement. He sighed and grunted in reply, "Okay. I'll go. I do need a stiff drink tonight. And the best ones in life are paid for by someone else."

By the time the sun had set that evening, Mirzya was regretting his decision, quite evidently made in a vulnerable moment and under pressure from Pawan.

I guess I will make the trip for the free booze and perhaps get some interesting gossip from the political circles. It could provide some fodder for my next film, Mirzya thought to himself, trying hard to see the silver lining.

The party was at a rather Tony luxury hotel where he met an assortment of ill-informed politicians looking for a good time and corporate honchos and *filmwalas* all eager to impress them. Mirzya felt depressed, but covered up his feelings admirably by speaking on international geopolitics, which emphasized his intellectual superiority over the company present. Of course, at the end of the ten-minute soliloquy, there was just Pawan left by his side looking rather anxious.

Mirzya decided to get himself a last drink at the bar. He downed a large single-malt and began plotting his exit when he felt as though there was someone standing right behind him.

Mirzya turned to see that it was the host, Purohit Pandey. Even in the dim light, Mirzya could see that Pandey's skin was waxen – effects of microdermabrasion – and his hair a carrot-red. *In trying to emulate film-star glamour these wannabes turn themselves into such caricatures*, Mirzya thought to himself.

Pandey addressed him directly with a polite smile. "I wanted to discuss something with you," he said with a quiet air of authority.

His curiosity piqued, Mirzya nodded an okay. Pandey steered him onto the hotel balcony overlooking the Arabian sea and the Sea-link.

Leaning against the balcony railing, Pandey cleared his throat and began to speak rather matter-of-factly, "My son Puttu wants to act in a film. But I want him to join politics. After all, he is my heir. He has agreed, but on one condition – that he gets to act in at least one legitimate film. Now, I have approached many top-line directors but they are very busy … blocked for at least the next five years, and I can't wait that long. Trust me, I know that he is a terrible actor and that this movie will flop, but I have to keep my promise to my only son and let him do that one film."

He paused to take a breath and check Mirzya's face for an expression of interest. Met with a stoic expressionless nod from Mirzya, Pandey continued regardless.

"And then it struck me that you, Mirzya bhai, would be the perfect director for him as your films don't have the pressure of commercial success. You make socially relevant films so that would be the safest bet. After all, I believe in social service. And too much romance or sex, or something trashy can really backfire on someone with political ambitions. Besides, your films are watched mostly in foreign countries and not in India, so not many here will really see it, which suits me fine. So do you have a project that is ready to roll immediately?"

Mirzya let all that sink in and was just about tipsy enough to begin to acquaint the gentleman about his artistic integrity when Pawan appeared by his side miraculously, like a genie out of a bottle. "Of course, minister sahab. *Mirzya bhai ke paas bilkul perfect script ready hai* – serious award-winning material."

Pandey scrunched his nose. "*Award-shaward aap log rakh lena. Bas meray Puttu ko achchi tarah film mein present kar dena.*"

Before Mirzya could interject, a meeting for the script narration had been fixed for the next afternoon – at yet another luxury hotel.

Mirzya was in a fix. His new script was complex and nuanced, and unlikely to be pulled off by a greenhorn, leave alone someone whose own doting and rather indulgent father had recognised and declared him a bad actor. Pawan, however, was undeterred. He kept reminding Mirzya that the offer was too tempting. Things were suddenly looking up and it would be foolish to knock aside a visit from Goddess Lakshmi herself.

After some persuasion, a barebones version of the original script was narrated to the father-son duo at the hotel over a seven-course meal and copious amounts of liquor, all of course, paid for by Pandey Sr.

Mirzya began the narration with his characteristic cold-open style. "The opening scene is in a dance bar. There is darkness all around, a glass shatters and as it comes into focus, you see the silhouette of the young man who has accidentally broken a bottle. Ajay is a street urchin who has grown up in the dark alleys of Mumbai and has learnt how lucrative selling liquor and drugs can be. It appears to be a far more attractive option than getting himself enrolled in a municipal college. In this introductory scene, he is in the bar to negotiate a deal with the bar's tough owner, Ramana Shetty, the only one in the area who is not purchasing booze from Ajay's gang of boys. After that we get into the background of a parallel distribution system of liquor, both legitimate and spurious, by enterprising youngsters who don't really have a shot at a good education or the big opportunities in life. And then eventually, despite his brilliance and enterprise, Ajay fails because the system is loaded against self-made people like him," Mirzya finished with a flourish, painting what he in his own mind thought was quite the picture.

"But this could set a wrong example. It could be disastrous for Puttu's political image. He can't be breaking the law. He should be a role model. No! Absolutely not. And bar is the worst place to open with," objected Pandey Sr.

Puttu Pandey, who had been listening intermittently, as he browsed through comments on his photos on Facebook, suddenly broke his silence. "Papaji, I don't mind the breaking-law part but it should start with a college scene ... so much darkness in the very beginning can put people off. We want brightness. We don't want another *andhera-wala* film from Andheri-based film-makers."

Puttu then extended his phone to show Mirzya a scene from *Godfather*, available on YouTube. "See, it's a gangster film but it still has a wedding scene," he pointed out gleefully.

Mirzya was trying to muster all the patience he could to prevent himself from bursting a blood vessel over Puttu's muddled expertise on film-making. Pawan gave him a pleading look. *We need this, we need this*, thought Pawan, hoping that Mirzya could somehow read his mind. Mirzya caught his eye and seemed to have understood.

Through clenched teeth he said, "Pandey-ji, this is just a movie. In fact, being a modern, poor young boy will make his young voters relate to him. And Puttu Beta, if we put you in a fancy, glossy college, it won't work because you are supposed to be a *poor* young man."

Pandey Sr smiled. He liked the idea of appealing to poor young voters – an ever-growing constituency and a pliant vote-bank. They were critical to his victory in the upcoming election. Dropping a generous sprinkling of gutkha in his mouth, he said, "*Haan theek hai lekin phir bhi gaali galauj kum aur bar scene mein vulgarity bilkul nahin honi chahiye. Actually nikaal hi doh toh better hai."*

"Par college scene is a must, papa. All big films about youngsters have college scenes," protested Puttu petulantly.

"Okay, okay. Let director sa'ab decide on the college scene," Pandey Sr said with an expression that conveyed that he actually didn't want it at all, but was reluctantly indulging his heir apparent.

Knowing Mirzya's tendency to almost always speak his mind, Pawan jumped in to salvage the situation.

"Arrey, Puttu-ji, *aap samjho, college scene ho gaya.* Mirzya sir is an expert in creating scenes and college scene is child's play for him."

Mirzya looked apoplectic, but given the situation that Pawan and his accountant had been continually reminding him of, he had no choice but to press on with the meeting.

Purohit Pandey was just warming up to the idea. "Dekhiye, money is no problem. This is my son's future. My son's launch should be no less than any other hero's son's launch … like Ranbir Kapoor or Shahid Kapoor's brother."

Mirzya rolled his eyes some more, but he knew he needed someone to bankroll his next film or his career was as good as over, never mind the accolades. *Awards will perhaps serve as good tombstones on the wasteland of my acclaimed films.*

With that epiphany, the conversation with the Pandeys suddenly felt more tolerable. He resorted to the tried-and-tested technique of responding with, "Yes, of course I can work that out," which didn't commit to specifics.

He reached deep inside himself and began to spin a new sort of story. The kind he had parodied in skits and student short-films at his elite film school. He warmed up and launched into the kind of freewheeling 'filmi' narration that he and his fellow custodians of serious, artistic cinema looked down upon as being the worst sort of ingredient of 'masala style of film-making'. Mirzya's Bollywoodsian flight of fancy had its desired effect. At the end of his narration, the Pandeys beamed from ear to ear, looking quite satisfied.

"We respect your kind of intelligent cinema. That's why after meeting the top-notch directors and rejecting them, we came to you," said Pandey Sr as he got up to leave.

Once the Pandeys rolled off in their fancy car, Mirzya turned to Pawan and had a long due and well-deserved apoplectic fit.

A few days later, he wrote what he believed was the worst script he had ever written and sent it across to the Pandeys. Much to his horror, it got greenlit almost immediately.

"The fastest ever in your career, sir," Pawan reminded him cheekily.

And thus it began, the filming of Mirzya's next film, *Student Leader*.

The first day of the shoot at Chand Bungalow in Madh Island went smoothly despite the shoot being disturbed a few times by the bunch of the Pandeys' family members and supporters who had landed up on the sets to watch their 'Puttu Babu' as hero. Phone cameras clicking selfies ruled over film cameras in those early days.

With stoic resignation, Mirzya attempted to bash on regardless of these creative challenges. Yoga between the shots helped him calm his nerves as also the occasional reefer in the afterhours. Puttu Pandey was sincere in the initial scenes given to him. But within a week, his confidence bolstered by his early success, Puttu decided to spring a surprise. To be precise, it was at the shoot of the aforementioned college scene that things got complicated.

As per the compromise plan with the Pandeys, Mirzya had introduced a college scene which was more an exchange of rebellious repartee in keeping with the hero's personality. It was when Pawan noticed Pandey Jr's blue contact lenses that he realized that things may not go as planned. But it was too late.

"This film will not work without a song," declared Puttu – preening for the film crew in a flashy pair of slashed denims and a tee that displayed his carefully sculpted body to advantage – to the flabbergasted Mirzya. "We need a song. So why not have a peppy campus number to increase the youth appeal?"

He had even hired a choreographer to design an impromptu flash mob-like song with Puttu in the centre surrounded by a bevy of girls.

Mirzya could not bear it. He rose from the director's chair and threw his microphone on the floor and walked off in a huff.

There was pindrop silence until Pawan had the presence of mind to call for a break and rush off to the director's vanity van.

Pawan found Mirzya holding his head in his hands, striking a tragic pose resembling Rodin's *Thinker*.

"C'mon, Mirzya sir. You have to resume the shoot. You have dealt with much worse," Pawan said firmly, like he would instruct a petulant child.

"I can't do it. I'd much rather hang my boots than work on these ghastly ideas I just committed to. What will people say?" shot back the agitated director.

Pawan knew that as a producer, it was only right that he should put his foot down to better the film's commercial prospects. But, he also knew Mirzya well enough not to take the direct approach.

"What has got into you, sir? Why do you care what people say. You are Mirzya Iman. Your film has gone to Cannes. You've had enough accolades to last a lifetime. Precious good have they done you apart from all those articles and write-ups. If you could convert all those articles into cash you could be a rich man. But, unfortunately you can't."

This last statement did make Mirzya think. Indeed, he had been lauded to the hilt, but was forced to beg and scrape for every new film of his.

Pawan sensed that Mirzya was calming down. Seizing the moment, he offered to take his boss for a long drive in the scenic parts of Madh Island to soothe his ruffled feathers.

For a while they drove in silence and then finally Pawan said, "Sir, I had an idea which I could discuss if you are open to hearing it."

Mirzya sulked some more in silence. Pawan realized it was a resigned 'yes', so he ventured forth.

"Sir, what if I supervised this song? If the film turns out to be very bad, I will take the blame, and you would then just be producer and presenter? As long as they see you on the set and know that your name is on the project, what do they really care? After all, this film is just about satisfying Puttu Pandey's itch before his father launches his political career. It is not your creative vision, so why not just sit back and make some money? I know you don't care for money, but if we get some big bucks from this project, even if it's the worst film in your filmography, you will be able to pay off the creditors and also buy your dream office in Versova. *Aap zara socho*, sir."

Pawan's words hit home. Mirzya had already received a hefty signing amount for the film and he was certainly not going to return that. But, he certainly wasn't going to let Pawan know that. Mirzya shot Pawan a scathing and disgusted glance. "Pawan, I don't know why you have this obsession with material things. But … Okay. Only because you are insisting so much."

Pawan heaved a sigh of relief. Having made sure that the advance monies had all come into the account in time, just in case Mirzya stopped shooting citing non-payment as an excuse, he felt a lot more relaxed. Now it was just about getting Mirzya on the sets. Their agreement with Pandey Sr stated that it had to be Mirzya who was directing the film, so orchestrating Pawan's own intervention had to be carefully thought through. Surprisingly it was Mirzya who provided the answer.

"I have accepted the idea of doing this film as God's will, Pawan. It is 'fate' accompli, as they say. I am bowing to the wishes of the Almighty," he told Pawan two days before they were to begin shooting.

Pawan, who had never been a staunch believer in God, suddenly saw the unquestionable powers of the Almighty and knew exactly how to explain Mirzya's absence on the sets for the song sequence. An expert at scheduling, he took the dates of the song and college scene shoot to Puttu and Pandey Sr and pointed out the big problem facing them.

"Sir, 3, 6 and 9 are incompatible for the combination of Puttu and Mirzya sir as per their birthdates. When we are pulling out all stops to make this film a success – imagine Mirzya sir has agreed to put a song and a college scene in the film – why take such a big risk? Pandey-ji, Puttu sir *ke future ka bhi sawaal hai*," he said to the Pandeys. After some serious deliberation with their very own pundit, they agreed.

From then on, things fell into a convenient pattern. Mirzya would come in and direct the parts that he had written and kept unaltered, while Pawan stepped in and directed the newly written, embarrassing bits which incorporated suggestions from Pandey Sr and the ever-innovative Puttu.

And God seemed to have heard his fervent prayers on behalf of both Mirzya and himself. With enough dates from the actor for retakes and reshoots, and because most of the filming was done in Mumbai, the film was finished in record time.

Mirzya almost had another breakdown at the editing table. He hated what he saw. "I can't believe the utter crap I have created," he screamed out loud. He wanted to leave the film's editing midway and escape to wash off the dirt and grime by taking in a few works of cinematic art at the Tallinn Black Nights Film Festival in Estonia. But, Pawan, who had turned into a very persuasive producer, refused to let him slink away. He would keep reminding Mirzya of his dream office and the very awful consequences – including being shot by unknown assassins hired by Puttu or Pandey Sr – that abandoning this project could bring about.

After an excruciating month of editing, Mirzya had a rough cut for distributors so that they would give it at least a few screens especially in the UP, Bihar, Central Provinces circuit – the domain of the Pandeys. The distributors were the hardcore, paan-chewing, white-pant-white-shirt, show-me-girls-and-guns-on-film-posters kind, definitely no fans of Mirzya's eclectic films.

With a faith that would have done a born-again devotee proud, Pawan had a priest perform an elaborate puja before the screening to get the distributors favourably disposed towards his debut-of-sorts. He even paid the priest a premium for gently putting into the ears of the believers his prediction for the film. "*Bahut mangal aur shubh samay mein release hai. Sab achcha hoga.*"

After the screening was over, Mirzya walked into screening room. He was greeted by an unexpected silence. Looking apologetic and the very picture of a tragic hero, Mirzya braced himself for the brickbats. He was quite sure that the distributors would hate the film. Shortly he would have Purohit Pandey on his doorstep asking for his head on a platter.

A few seconds later, Duru Bhai, one of the biggest distributers in north India, stood up and exclaimed loudly, "Mirzya sahib, *finally aapne arty-farty picture chhod ke ek commercial picture bana hi daali.* There is no star appeal, *par aajkal aisi achchi content wali film pasand karte hain log.* And the dark humour will work very well. *Aapki pictures nahin toh bahut serious hoti thi.* This is a comedy and even families might enjoy it. Picture hit *ho sakti hai.*"

Mirzya could not believe his ears. Here he was, surrounded by hardcore masala-film distributors showering accolades on him for making the transition! At first he was tongue-tied but soon his director's quick-to-the-draw instincts kicked in.

"Of course, one has to reinvent oneself to stay relevant."

Student Leader had a modest release but given its reasonable production budget and good word-of-mouth from trade pundits, it turned into the unexpected, surprise sleeper hit of the season.

As for the Pandeys, they were happy with Puttu Pandey's gritty portrayal of the young firebrand youth leader, who, in keeping with Hindi film hero traditions, could also break into a dance if required. And yes, according to the new 'Hero', the ladies were absolutely swooning over him.

Mirzya humbly claimed all the glory that comes with success. For the first time in his career he behaved in true-blue Bollywood manner and had a grand 'success party'. Ayaaz Khan graced the party, carrying a six-foot-tall flower bouquet and asked Mirzya to make his next film with him.

As an aside, Mirzya also announced that he would produce a film which Pawan would direct and yes, that swanky dream office in Andheri is under construction even as you read this.

Baby Boon

IS BLUE BAY HOSPITAL THE NEW HATCHERY FOR STAR BABIES?

Dr Satpathy, the CEO of Blue Bay Hospital, smiled, amused by the headline. *Newspapers these days* ... he thought to himself. He would much rather the hospital made news about the competence of the staff and their medical feats than such frivolity, but on the bright side, it would keep them in business, and then some more. He was quite proud of his hospital and his team, and approved of good things being said of them.

He was sipping his morning cuppa in his cabin on the second floor of the hospital, thinking of ways to raise the bar further for his celebrity clients. Through the massive French windows in front of him he could see the sizeable crowd of camerapersons swarming around below at the entrance for photos of the star babies that had made well-publicized entries into 'tinsel town'. His thoughts went to his favourite baby celebrities who had catapulted the hospital into such prominence. Superstar Samrat Kumar's glorious parenthood was followed within a week by Jay Khanna's babies. The tabloids and gossip sites couldn't have asked for more. Sure, he was concerned about traffic snarls right outside the hospital as also the nuisance value of hospital staff getting tempted into sharing information with the media. But he'd get around to figuring how to deal with them later. For now, he just wanted to enjoy the moment of glory. It was after a lot of work that Blue Bay Hospital had become a favourite with jet-setting celebrities.

*

The photographers parked on the road seemed frustrated with their vigil. They were constantly jostling each other for better photo-capturing positions. A family-oriented photograph, such as the one presented by this rare and momentous occasion, had wider appeal on the Internet, translating into more takers which meant better income for them. The smarter photographers camping at the site for the last two days had invested in sophisticated zoom/tele lenses so that they could get photos of the visiting film stars, even from vantage points in neighbouring buildings.

Someone piped up, "Arrey! Jay Khanna's car!"

A black Hummer had just zoomed into the driveway. The sight of the car immediately galvanized the mass of photographers into action.

Jay Khanna, unmistakably himself in a whacky ensemble of a colourful dhoti and a T-shirt with cute teddy bears printed on it, alighted from the vehicle along with his mother. Frenzied shouts of "Jay, please look this way," broke out, interspersed with camera flashes. He waved cursorily at the photographers and rushed towards the hospital entrance.

Then, in trademark style he stopped dramatically, turned, performed a crazy cartwheel and then with a whoop of joy blew kisses in the direction of the cameras. "*Mera promotion ho gaya, bhai log*," he shouted cheerfully.

A newbie journalist ran up to him with a mike. "Jay, do you have anything to say about the fact that you and Samrat Kumar chose the same hospital for your babies? Is it because you have a legendary rivalry with him?"

Jay smiled at the journalist indulgently. "There is no rivalry between Samrat Kumar and me. There never has been. And there never will be." Saying this he winked mischievously before marching off into the hospital.

*

Contrary to what Jay Khanna said, his rivalry with Samrat Kumar was the stuff of Bollywood legend.

Samrat Kumar, a strapping handsome man with the chiselled good looks of a Greek God, was unmatchable in his screen presence. He was also a nimble dancer and stunning in action sequences – features that made him a crowd favourite and a huge success at the box office. His life was as much the fairy-tale life as could be. To the manor born, he had a happy family life and a long Bollywood ancestry. His wife was his childhood sweetheart, also from showbiz aristocracy. The gods had been kind to them. But of late, the audience had turned fickle. And Samrat had to bend over backwards to keep them interested in his life and work.

Samrat Kumar's family hailed from north India, a part of erstwhile west-Punjab that now belonged to Pakistan.

His grandfather had risen through the ranks after working in a cinema hall and then catering for film crews before he became a producer himself. He launched his son as an actor and the latter had achieved middling success but with Samrat, they had delivered to every audience expectation and rapidly risen to the top of the Bollywood heap and stayed there ever since.

Samrat was a private person but given his picture-perfect life and glamorous family members, each as good looking as the other, he made headlines effortlessly. Always immaculate, not a hair out of place. He looked almost unreal. Some used the word fake or plastic but that was perhaps too unkind. Samrat was just made that way, so perfect that one could sometimes pass him off for bland and borderline dull.

Given his upbringing within the family folds and very limited exposure to a world outside of movie shoots, heroes, heroines and the world of make-believe, Samrat could sound unaware and out of touch with goings-on in the world outside Bollywood. It was ironic that he could say the most ludicrous lines on screen with panache but when it came to saying something to a real fan in real life, he was at a complete loss for words.

While his fans could see no fault in his ever-courteous and chivalrous persona, the cynics thought it was all a sham. Fortunately for Samrat, the latter theory had very few takers.

Jay Khanna was a complete contrast to Samrat. Almost a decade ago, he had landed in Mumbai with a dream. One that a million others nurtured and came to this *maya-nagri* for. Jay was average looking with an inexplicable, earthy sort of appeal. He was also very well-read, had trained as an engineer, studied in a premier business institute, before he ended up in the wonderland called Bollywood. His success, although it did not come overnight like Samrat's, had been no less dazzling. When you are the Average Joe in the looks department, not from an elite family and have a rival that makes men and women swoon at the sight of his rippling physique, there is only one thing you can do – be better than the best at your job along with nurturing a generous amount of quirkincss.

Towards this end, Jay had decided to compensate for his plain looks by creating a fashion frenzy with outlandish ensembles. It had all started when one fine day Jay stepped out of his building in a wide flared skirt and a kurta. The paparazzi hanging around star bungalows, tired of their thankless duty, couldn't have enough. He had given them a new *paisa-wasool* shot. It was rare to get anything beyond cars with dark windows rolled up in the posh Bandra pocket borough. Predictably, the photo made its way to all leading papers. And since then, Jay rarely failed to disappoint. "Outlandish becomes me," was a favourite line that he dropped whenever he made appearances adorned in his wild new wardrobe experiments. The media loved his crazy fashion antics. To add to this Jay began to get very experimental with his roles and projects. All of thirty-five, he had established himself as an 'intelligent actor'. "Intelligence is super sexy," he would say at every given opportunity to his growing legion of fans.

In sharp contrast to Samrat's politically correct poise, Jay's quirky narrative, often topsy-turvy and unpredictable, was always a topic of discussion for a long time.

The two men had been traversing their own parallel tracks, aware of each other but not really involved in each other's lives till the inevitable happened. Their paths collided. At a party hosted by senior film stalwart Dev Kumar, the two stars arrived at the same time. Or at least within a few seconds of each other. Samrat was posing for the cameras – his wife and he made a striking visual. It was going swimmingly well and Samrat was almost politely begging to be let off while the photographers kept insisting for just 'one more photo'. And that's when Jay arrived in a glittering golden suit complete with a cherry-red top hat! His outfit was so outlandish and blingy that almost immediately the focus shifted. The cameras all turned towards Jay to capture him in all his ridiculous glory. Samrat was stupefied for a minute. It was an excruciatingly long moment. To Samrat it felt as though suddenly the world had forgotten him.

Jay knew that he had to own the room with an antic or two the moment he walked in. Intuitive as ever, in a blink, before Samrat could gather his wits, Jay milked the opportunity to the hilt. After his solo '*poster phaad ke nikla hero*' entry, he walked over to the gorgeous couple and began to pose for photographs with Samrat and his wife, looking all friendly and pally. There was a feeding frenzy among the photographers and Samrat and his wife were forced to stay and pose for another ten minutes as Samrat didn't want to leave Jay alone and steal the moment.

Samrat was really cut up with Jay for stealing his thunder that night. As it was, he could never quite understand these flashy and desperate newbie types with their crazy antics because he never had to really struggle for attention. It came to him rather effortlessly. As did work. But word had reached him through friends and managers that Jay was now approaching his friends, top-notch directors and producers, promising to work for them for half of what Samrat's fee would be. Most had laughed it off but one or two had been tempted. Kalash Pictures had already signed him up for three films as had Good Fortune Films.

Samrat had, of course, with the help of his extended Bollywood family quickly got into damage-control mode, making overtures to old and new, unblocking dates and making himself accessible to a few he had stonewalled over the past few years. His family's deep connects and goodwill always helped him and he even landed a plum project with an international studio that had been considering Jay for their maiden film in India. However, Samrat knew that Jay was neck-to-neck with him in the race and might soon overtake him.

And it was around then that their mutual discomfort with each other had turned into official and cutthroat rivalry.

Jay's popularity had soared among the young city-bred millennial brigade who lapped up his Bohemian style. A few popularity and power lists put out by magazines and websites had begun ranking Jay ahead of Samrat. *CelebRated*, the most coveted and followed among these lists, was the first to peg Jay Khanna in the '30 under 30' stars to watch out for. Samrat's PR team was immediately at work to find out how this had happened. His trusted lieutenant Maina came back with classified info – Jay had been wining and dining the editors, especially Anamika, the editor of *CelebRated*. In fact, a close common friend had confirmed to Samrat that Jay had had a fling with Anamika too! Samrat was informed by his trusted allies that this alleged proximity was why Samrat had been knocked down to a lower position.

All this would not have bothered Samrat so much if his film *#Shaadi*, a family drama aimed at millennials, had worked its magic with the young audience. Unfortunately, it had tanked, while a raucous comedy titled *Bachelor Boys*, starring Jay with a bunch of newbie actors, had struck gold, making him a youth icon of sorts.

Samrat knew he couldn't sit back and watch any longer. The manipulation of the *CelebRated* list by Jay Khanna meant that the war had begun. He was damned if he would let himself be upstaged by such a pedestrian actor, a Johnny-come-lately. To borrow from Jay's extensive list of clever quips, "All is fair in Star Wars."

Samrat's publicist swung into action and immediately whispered to a network of trusted journalists always eager for a scoop that there was talk about Jay Khanna being gay! "*A young self-made star whose last film was a big success has painted himself in the image of a Casanova that he is not. At least, his interests do not lie in the opposite sex. Buzz in Tinseltown suggests that the young star is partial to gentlemen and not ladies. Well, in this day and age, there is no shame in owning your sexuality and certainly not for someone as unconventional as him. Wonder when he will share his secret with the world.*"

This was just one among a dozen such 'blind items' that fanned the speculation of the unwarranted kind for Jay Khanna.

*

Jay Khanna got a whiff of the conspiracy being hatched when his stylist, Raoul, heard the Chinese whispers about his client from his boyfriend.

"Jay, did you know that we are supposed to be a ménage à trois?" he said jokingly to Jay when they were getting him ready for a photo-shoot.

Jay, after goofily serenading Raoul, sat down for a smoke, his mind racing on what he had just heard. He could see himself being declared unfit to play the romantic hero roles, given his rumoured sexual orientation. He knew this one lie could mean the death of his career.

He had never been one to grudge others their success. As an active sportsman during his college days, Jay Khanna strongly believed that the best man should win. He had a vague idea of how this had transpired but wanted to be sure before he decided his course of action. Jay preferred an open fight or show of aggression to a sneaky, innuendo-laden whisper campaign. His foe Samrat, however, was all for the cloak-and-dagger game.

Smile and be a villain, thought Jay bitterly to himself, recalling how warm and effusive Samrat had seemed afterwards at the party where they had posed together for the paparazzi. Why, Samrat had even invited Jay over to his house for drinks afterwards. And followed up this bout of congeniality by posting a selfie with Jay on Instagram which had become witness and proof of the camaraderie they had shared that night. That night, Jay had felt that at last he had been accepted as an equal by the blue-blooded set. But obviously it was not that way at all. It had all been a charade. Jay, however, realized that at this time silence was golden. So, he just decided to keep a low profile for a few days.

A few days later, Jay went to Blue Bay Hospital where he had to see Dr Satpathy for a small meet-and-greet activity he had agreed to with children suffering from cancer and while at it, also slip in an innocuous query on stress-induced health hazards. The doctor was easy to chat with and had convinced Jay that participating in the noble cause was "the best therapy for the rich and the famous". No wonder he was a favourite with celebrities. He knew just how to keep them happy. Pampering them like kids and behaving as though he had all the time and sympathy for a lot of their inconsequential problems. His film star patients ended up confiding in the doctor ever so often.

"Hi doc, how are you? Just been having these anxiety spells but I don't want to take any medication. What would you recommend?" Jay didn't believe in beating about the bush.

"Young man, I would suggest settling down and growing your family. A work–life balance is important no matter how busy you may be with work. Learn from your friend Samrat. He's almost come around to the idea after much persuasion," the good doctor advised.

Jay's ears immediately perked up although he kept a straight face. "So, what's it that Samrat is coming around to?" he asked, trying to sound as casual as he could.

"I'm sure Samrat will share it with you when he's ready," replied the doctor, changing the topic. "But right now let's focus on the solution to your problem. As I said earlier, no medication, just meditation and some work as a Good Samaritan should help. Although we will have our best doctor discuss it with you. Meanwhile, our favourite nurse, Sister Swati, as always, will accompany you to the children's ward. They are eagerly awaiting your storytelling session with them."

Jay decided to drop the subject with the doctor who got busy summoning Sister Swati to the room. "Sister, do accompany Mr Khanna on his children-ward visit. I am busy right now but will try to catch up in a bit."

"Hi Sister, how are you? Every time we meet, I can see that your halo has become brighter, with all the good work you do," Jay said as he accompanied her out. Sister Swati, a rather pleasant-looking young lady, beamed as she noticed Dr Satpathy nod in approval at Jay's statement.

With niceties out of the way, Jay sprung the question that was foremost on his mind on their way upstairs. He knew that after that glowing compliment before her boss, Sister Swati would certainly give him all the juicy details.

"My friend Samrat is such a family man, happily married and all that … what was he hesitating about?" he asked casually.

"How can I say all that … especially given all your rivalry?" Sister Swati demurred.

"Sister, all that is drama for the media! Let me show you our rivalry," said Jay, scrolling to the photo of him with Samrat and his wife at Dev Kumar's party. The three definitely looked like best buddies.

As Sister Swati gazed approvingly at the photo on the phone screen, Jay, in a dramatic swoop, took the palm of her hand and kept it on his chest. "Honestly, Sister, do I look like someone with such a small heart?"

Blushing a bright red, butterflies in her stomach, Sister Swati lowered her voice and whispered, "Oh, he had a big argument with his poor wife when he discovered that she was pregnant. She wants the child. He doesn't."

"No! I don't believe it," Jay exclaimed, feigning shock and horror.

"Actually, Samrat and his wife had a fight inside the private maternity ward room during his wife's check-up. It really was quite ugly, my ward boy recorded it on his phone just for kicks. It's in extremely bad taste too. He played it and made me hear it," she whispered conspiratorially.

Jay stopped in his tracks and looked at Sister Swati in mock horror. "That is a terrible thing to do, Sister. Did you delete it?"

Noticing that her pretty face looked troubled, he added, "Don't worry, why don't you ask him to forward it to you? And maybe I'll ask my techie friends to delete it from the source. He can possibly hack into it or something. You do know that this could get you into a lot of trouble. Why, you could even lose your job because as supervisor, you cannot let it happen on your watch."

Sister Swati looked a little doubtful, but only briefly. She loved Jay – who didn't? – and judging by the way he had behaved towards her in all their interactions until now she knew he had a good heart. Imagine, going out of his way to ensure that some ordinary nurse did not lose her job.

"That boy is trouble. He did not listen to me when I asked him to delete it. Is it possible for your friend to do it? I don't want to lose my job. Please? I promise, I will return the favour any way that I can," she said.

"Of course, Sister Swati. I would never let you come in harm's way. Consider the job done. Let's focus now on our storytelling session with the kids," said Jay.

*

Samrat was having a sleepless night. His wife's unplanned pregnancy had got him worried.

It was too early in his career to be saddled with a child. Getting married itself had been a matter of debate. He had always felt that it had impacted his 'heart-throb' status somewhat. But now, being a father so soon could put him in jeopardy again. From Adonis, he could land straight in the 'uncle' category which was a major concern for his film producers.

But what was really bugging Samrat was a nagging doubt. He wasn't sure if the child was his own. The date of conception did not add up. He recalled he was shooting in London at the time for an international film in which he'd landed an important ensemble part. And because he wanted to have a fling with a British actress working on the film, he'd lied to his wife and told her that the studio had made him sign a 'no wives and girlfriends on location' clause in his contract. His wife had a hard time believing this, but with some persuasion she had given him the benefit of doubt and not accompanied him. But when he had returned, something in the way she came across had given Samrat a sneaky feeling that she may have cheated on him in turn. Of course, he could not really articulate his doubts or put the suspicion to test. If the child was not Samrat's own, it would be terrible for his image to show the world that he had been cuckolded. It was far more convenient and logical to put down his reluctance to be a father to his career concerns. The only hitch was his parents' excitement and insistence on a grandchild! After consultation with the family astrologer, producers, his agency etc., the family had all weighed in favour of expanding the family.

Samrat's father and uncle had come up with a strategy to take care of Samrat's concerns about his image. Family, after all, was certainly Samrat's trump card. India was all about family and everyone in Samrat's family was a celebrity or a quasi-celeb. Why, all Samrat and his brood had to do was get together for coffee and put up the photo for it to become an Internet rage. Samrat's family's image worked wonders for him, so why not capitalize on that and become a true blue 'family man'?

According to 'research' done by Samrat's manager, the threat from Jay's rising stardom could be negated using Samrat's new 'family man' positioning. It was an advantage that Jay could never compete with. He was unmarried and his bohemian ways might appear charming to the media but hardly impressed the people of real India.

Jay came from an unknown, nondescript business family in the north. He had to work hard on keeping himself in news. And Jay had vowed that he would never give up his wild ways for the sake of getting married. "Marriage is an outdated concept which has long outlived its utility or purpose of being a licence for having sex! I am not giving up my great life just for that," Jay had famously declared in celebrity magazine interviews time and again.

Samrat's manager was convinced that an additional Kumar in the family was the best thing to happen at this juncture of his career. It would pull in the advertising with various multinational baby and family products and brands who were eager to 'explore opportunities'.

And so began the PR blitzkrieg. Instagram photos of Samrat taking care of his wife, them goofing around, pajama parties, *gode bharai* and so on flooded myriad timelines. The brands loved it and everyone from Pink Pajamas, Royal Paints, Baby Basket to jewellery brands lined up to sign Samrat Kumar in a never-seen-before avatar. But the biggest of them all was a top international luxury car brand which wanted to sign up for being the official 'bring home the baby vehicle'.

In terms of visibility, it was hard to miss Samrat with the carpet bombing of media coverage and ads that were created around the impending arrival. This was a godsend. They had taken the right decision. His next film was due soon and this visibility was like free publicity in building the momentum.

*

Jay too had his own battles to fight in order to win the game. His strategy was to bend backwards to make him as exciting or a more exciting proposition than Samrat Kumar. In order to please the big guns, he had signed up for a lot of work for a lower price, both for films and advertisements. But a big chunk of brand endorsements which earned stars big bucks was still going to Samrat Kumar as Jay was seen as too unconventional!

And then came the fateful meeting at the Chambers in Beau Monde, the poshest of hotels in the city where the jetsetters meet. Jay along with his manager Shruti had opted for it for a hush-hush meeting with Vikas Grover, marketing head of Fit & Fun Foods Company, the biggest packaged food company in India. Jay had been a brand ambassador for the last three years and with his contract nearing the end of the tenure, it seemed like the perfect opportunity to renew old ties. In fact, Shruti had told him that from the gossip she had picked up from the marketing team, it was almost certain that Jay would get an extension.

"Grover Sa'ab, how are you, sir? *Kabhi hamare liye bhi time nikaal liya kijiye*," Jay pumped up the charm offensive.

"Arrey, you are the big star ... I have all the time in the world," replied Grover no mean player in the flattery game.

After some delicious appetizers had been washed down with the choicest French wines, and the mood was mellow, Jay decided to mix business with pleasure.

"Vikas, you and the team are like family to me – you know that – and I am looking forward to continuing my association with Fit & Fun Foods. So, let's drink to that!" he said, embracing Vikas in a big bear hug.

After some awkward laughter, Vikas said, "Cheers, Jay! About the brand ambassador thing, I will be upfront with you. We had planned to sign up with you, but our most recent surveys show Samrat Kumar as a better fit for the positioning of this product which is for the entire family."

"But my association with the brand gave you guys such great visibility and connect with the youth," Jay stammered, looking crestfallen.

"Of course it did, which is why you were our first choice but then these surveys came up! And that rumour about you being gay did not help. What can we do, we are slaves to the consumer and as the saying goes, 'consumer is king'!" replied Grover.

It was with great difficulty that Jay sat through the rest of the meeting but after a generous amount of wine and good food, he extracted enough information from Vikas Grover to understand that besides the consumer choice, Samrat had also generously offered to slash his fee!

Jay Khanna, for once feeling outsmarted, knew it was time to go for the jugular just the way his rival had gone for his.

*

The countdown to Samrat's Big Day was marked with a flurry of announcements, which continued unabated over the week.

Samrat Kumar pens a fond note to welcome his baby.

Samrat Kumar personally designed the nursery for his baby.

Netizens think Samrat Kumar will make the perfect father.

Samrat was feeling chuffed with all the headlines. He had never imagined that fatherhood would prove to be such a boon. Why, he had even got an offer from an international studio for playing the lead in a remake of their Hollywood film as a young, single father saddled with daddy duties that he was clueless about. This film would be made in multiple Indian languages and dubbed in Chinese too with an eye on the big China market, besides a release in other countries around the world. Samrat still didn't care much for the baby, but it was sure proving to be his lucky mascot!

Meanwhile, Jay Khanna was off the headlines. He had been keeping a very low profile almost as though he had taken a sabbatical. No crazy antics, no grand announcements. Nothing.

And then one fine morning, all hell broke loose. What followed was also something that nobody could have imagined.

An audio of Samrat Kumar having a meltdown at the Blue Bay Hospital about the baby not being his own suddenly exploded on the Internet.

To say that this was a bolt from the blue would be an understatement. Nobody, least of all Samrat, had expected his outburst at the hospital to have been recorded and to make its way to social media.

That night, the news was all about Samrat Kumar's irresponsible outburst. The panel discussions got angrier and memes crueller. Overnight, Samrat's legion of fans turned against him. Unfollowing and blocking him while some made their thoughts about his behaviour well known. The tide of negativity just refused to abate. #BoycottSamratKumar trended for days across social platforms.

Samrat's team issued many a stout denial but the audio stood as evidence against everything he said. The damage was done. Fit & Fun Foods was the first brand to pull away from any association from Samrat Kumar. Other brands followed suit and thus began the exodus prompting the quick departure of many friends, followers and film-makers.

Meanwhile, on the sidelines of this cataclysmic event, Jay Khanna made an amazing and unexpected announcement. He'd just had twins through surrogacy. He thanked the surrogate mother who remained anonymous (her identity was never disclosed, but some sources said that it was a nurse at the Blue Bay Hospital who had very graciously offered to have Jay's babies for an undisclosed sum).

Jay also thanked Dr Satpathy and Blue Bay Hospital for helping him bring into this world not one, but two bundles of joy – both girls whom he would give absolute equal opportunities without any gender discrimination.

Jay Khanna and his twins quickly became the toast of town as an example of the 'modern Indian family'. Jay was hailed and feted on all woke platforms. Millennials across various walks of life once again began celebrating and honouring the actor. He immediately made it to *India Now* magazine's list of the 'Most Powerful & Influential'!

And yes, for the grand unveiling and announcement of the list awards, Jay Khanna and the babies arrived in all their finery, with nannies in tow, in a fancy luxury car which had once been promised to Samrat Kumar for bringing his baby home.

As they say, there is no greater boon or blessing than a baby!

Director Bhola Bhala

Sunjoy Grover's office was abuzz with activity. It was only recently that he had launched his own production banner, Zeus Films, and moved into this brand-new space. There were just a handful of employees, mostly young creative assistants who, at that given moment were using their time well, working simultaneously on their laptops and talking in hushed whispers outside the sound-proofed conference room where Sunjoy was cloistered with key members of his team.

Sunjoy was in the middle of an important script session for the next film, also the first project under his own banner. Besides the fact that this was a special project, in Sunjoy's scheme of things, script discussions were a sacred process. Staff members from all departments got a seat at the table in the early stages and then gradually it was whittled down to the one or two who were actually working on the project along with Sunjoy. His painstaking attention to the script and storytelling was famous as the mantra for his enviable success. After all, Sunjoy Grover was among Bollywood's most successful directors and oddly enough, one whom everyone liked.

In fact, his gentlemanly manner and polite nature had even earned him a term of endearment: Director Bhola Bhala. Such was his track record that almost every respectable professional in showbusiness wanted to work with him. The biggest heroines of Bollywood were trying to entice him with their charms and Bollywood's hunkiest He-men were ready to work at half their commercial price – all for Sunjoy to use his Midas touch and deliver a super-duper hit with them starring in it.

Despite Sunjoy's strict standing instructions of do-not-disturb-under-any-circumstances, Ram, Sunjoy's executive assistant, barged into the conference room. He had his phone in his hand with the speaker cupped. "I know I am interrupting, Sunjoy sir, but Navin Sir is on fire. He's been giving me *ma-behen ki gaalis* on the phone for the past half hour. He wants to talk to you right now."

Navin Sir aka Navin Kishor Gupta was Sunjoy's mentor. The larger-than-life Bollywood film director–producer with whom Sunjoy had worked for the longest time – fifteen years and five blockbuster hits! Navin had recently and quite amicably cut the umbilical cord binding them, urging Sunjoy to strike out independently and launch his own production house.

Although it was Navin Sir on the phone, Sunjoy was still annoyed as hell at the intrusion. He hated being interrupted in the middle of script sessions. It just broke his creative flow, the train of cinematic thoughts. But then again, this was Navin who had the persistence and patience of a fruit-fly when he wanted something. And Navin was certainly not accustomed to his favourite protégé not answering his calls on a priority basis. Sunjoy glanced at his phone and saw at least fifty missed calls from Navin. That didn't bode well. He immediately snatched the phone that Ram was extending.

Navin's loud voice boomed into his ear, "Where are you, man? It's urgent. I could not get through to you so I am on my way to your office. Just a few seconds."

As he disconnected and dismissed the script session, Sunjoy could feel the butterflies in his stomach. This was most unusual. Navin knew how difficult it was to reach Sunjoy once he got into scripting sessions with co-writers. It must be something very urgent, and judging by Navin's tone, it wasn't going to be anything pleasant.

Sunjoy could always gauge Navin's mood by the tone of his voice. With his sudden bursts of energy and often unintended humour, Navin could always be relied upon to lighten up the mood. Especially, during the script sessions they used to have. This one time they had a narration with a superstar at his grand bungalow, full of precious crystalware and statues, a dangerous place to let Navin loose in. And sure enough, with his wild gesticulation of hands, he had soon landed a beautiful green Italian glass fruit bowl on the floor. The crash stunned everyone into silence but not Navin.

"Arrey yaar, put this too in the production budget. If there's something left over after your fees are paid, we will compensate for this!" Navin said with a nonchalant laugh. Anyone else in his place would have probably fallen at the hosts' feet and begged for forgiveness but Navin was something else.

Just recalling the incident brought a smile to Sunjoy's face. He figured that perhaps he could regroup the assistants later and even include Navin in his script session. On the bright side, an impromptu fun team session could transpire, never mind that the clock was ticking on his schedule.

Within a few minutes, Navin was in Sunjoy's cabin. He looked grim, a rare expression on his face. Ram poked his head in to ask for coffee but Sunjoy waved him away abruptly and closed the door.

"You are a good creative director, Sunjoy, but you can't hold your drinks, can you?" Navin hollered, thc disapproval quite evident in his voice.

Sunjoy stared blankly at him wondering where the conversation was headed.

"Erm, I've cut down on my drinking ... now it's only when I'm among friends. What's the matter?" Sunjoy stammered.

"*Abey yeh dekh*," Navin said, showing Sunjoy his phone. Focusing with great difficulty without his reading glasses, Sunjoy attempted to read out messages from someone titled Surabhi. The words sprang out at him but none of it was making sense. Till Navin broke in, "At that party we had a few days ago to celebrate the inauguration of your own production, you, Mister Sunjoy, got piss drunk and according to this young actress, Surabhi, who is part of the new talent under my banner, you misbehaved with her. She says you pawed her and tried to force her into the bathroom with you. How could you be so irresponsible? And on one of the biggest days of your life, yaar?"

Sunjoy was in shock. Truth be told, he did go on a drinking spree that night after a long, dry spell, and had only a hazy recollection about that party. Normally, for such parties he always had either his wife Renu or his assistant

Ram by his side. But Renu had to fly off to Delhi that night for a family emergency and Ram had an urgent booty-call to attend to, so had left quite early. Left to himself, Sunjoy had downed one drink too many.

Sunjoy tried hard to recall all that he did at the party. The last he remembered, he was indeed talking to a group of young talent, the starry-eyed young actors and actresses Navin's banner had signed up for films and web series. Sunjoy was having trouble processing what Navin had just laid on him. He had no memory of misbehaving with anyone. But then he also did not remember how he had got home that night. The next morning, he had risen with a bad hangover and had been blank about some parts of the previous night's party.

Filmi parties were a bit of a bone of contention between Renu and Sunjoy. Renu would get exasperated with the desperate efforts of the young ones trying to trip each other to get Sunjoy's attention. Sunjoy being the epitome of politeness engaged in conversation with everyone who came up to him. As a result, Renu felt left out and ignored.

This one time at a party, Renu, who was sitting right next to Sunjoy, was absolutely appalled when an actress, looking sexy as hell, slid into a seat next to him on the other side, ostensibly to say hello, and then refused to leave his side the entire evening. Much to Renu's annoyance, she kept fussing over Sunjoy, leaning across strategically to display her attractive cleavage. Sunjoy had been too flummoxed to react beyond uttering niceties and smiling politely. Renu was mad as hell with Sunjoy for not putting the actress in her place and getting rid of her. Finally, Renu had declared that she would not accompany Sunjoy to filmi parties.

After much discussion and pleading on Sunjoy's part, it was Renu who eventually figured a way out. It was decided that Renu would go to the important parties only. For all other sundry get-togethers, Sunjoy would be accompanied by Ram. An important part of Ram's job profile was to keep unwarranted attention at bay. All this of course was after Renu extracted a promise from Sunjoy that he would not succumb to any temptation that came his way.

The arrangement had worked well. Up until now.

Sunjoy was a little hurt at Navin's accusatory words, but he appreciated that Navin had given the news to him in confidence. Navin had always been upfront with him and never sugar-coated anything. Theirs was an unusual association by industry standards. And Navin had given Sunjoy a shot at every film person's big dream. Sunjoy was from a small town and had risen through the ranks, first as a cinematographer and then a director. He was fortunate to have found a mentor in Navin. Everybody asked Sunjoy why he hadn't struck out independently after his super-hit hat-trick. How could he allow Navin to soak up the spotlight and rake in the moolah?

Truth be told, Sunjoy, for the longest time, had preferred it that way. He was happy working behind the scenes without worrying about the commercial circus that making a film involved. Meeting distributors from different film-viewing circuits who were sharp as hell when it came to what made money but could not look beyond the 'saleable' elements was something Sunjoy found exasperating. He preferred to focus on the creative side of things. But, having come up the hard way, he was no artistic fool. He wanted his films to be *paisa-wasool* for the audience, but he wanted to do it his way. Not paint along the dots put down by film trade.

Navin was the perfect foil for Sunjoy. Quite the masala-style auteur himself despite the fact that his last film was made in the mid-1990s, Navin had reinvented himself as a producer and became an answer to Sunjoy's prayers. A master negotiator, he would always leave the table with a win-win deal. His family was well versed in the ways of the business. He could talk the talk to convince distributors and financiers. Something Sunjoy could not. He had also given Sunjoy his big break in the movies to make that switch from a cinematographer to a director. A huge leap of faith. And Sunjoy always felt he owed him one. Spotting the potential in him, Navin had convinced stars who were friends to act in Sunjoy's first film, *Amriki Sapne*. The film had a dream run and there was no looking back ever since.

Tempting offers kept coming his way but somehow Sunjoy dodged them with admirable focus. There was that one time when a superstar had made Sunjoy a proposal too hard to resist.

"Let me produce a film for you, and you come on board as co-producer. Navin is a friend and I adore him but you know how egoistical he is. He will never let you emerge from his shadow. I am different. *Main star hoon*. If I promote a director, he doesn't overshadow me, so I am not insecure. You have given Navin a lot. Now it's time you do something for yourself. You are the golden goose of his banner and now you are the reason why stars like me entertain him and not the other way round," the superstar had enthusiastically proposed.

Sunjoy had not been able to sleep that night. He had tossed and turned and told Renu about the conversation. Renu heard him out impatiently. She hated how Sunjoy, otherwise a master narrator of stories, could drone on and on about important stuff instead of getting to the point. Especially when he was feeling guilty about something. She heard him out and immediately understood why.

Sunjoy was guilt-tripped by the fact that he had even considered the suggestion. Sometimes she wondered how her forty-two-year-old husband had even succeeded in this cut-throat industry. As she asked this question out loud, both echoed the same answer: "Because of Navin!" They sat back on the bed laughing. That is what the right thing would be. To stay the course with Navin.

The next morning, he had gone to Navin's plush residence in Juhu and informed him of the offer, assuring him that he had declined. Navin hugged him and said Sunjoy was like his own brother. Sunjoy was relieved. He had made the right decision. Navin was family and like he had said, there would be more and better opportunities. They laughed, had a cup of tea, and abused film stars who thought the world of themselves.

"Yaar, when the time is ripe I will myself ask you to start your own production independently," Navin had said in a voice choked with emotion and hugged Sunjoy.

And so Sunjoy had made two more superhits under Navin's banner. Financially, Sunjoy had done well. But Navin had done better, especially by wearing the producer's hat and "taking all the risks!"

But then, a few months ago, Navin had sat him down for a heart-to-heart and convinced him that he was ready to fly the nest. Truth be told, it was not just Navin. With five successful films with his credit only as director, Sunjoy had been thinking about it too. The last project they had worked on had witnessed many a flare-up between them. In fact, Sunjoy had been directly meeting film stars who were sending out feelers to him, because he now felt he was equipped to take certain creative and even business decisions instead of Navin forcing his hand. Sunjoy was certain that he wanted his next project to be grand with shoots in foreign locations to match the impressive star cast and yes, possibly a better technical and music team than Navin's favourites.

Alas, now when the time had come to finally get out of Navin's shadows, it appeared as though Sunjoy might have messed up big-time.

He snapped back to the present. Navin was saying something to him. "The media will crucify you for this. And as for your family life..."

"Please don't tell Renu. She will be devastated," Sunjoy pleaded, almost falling at Navin's feet. "Do something, Navin-bhai."

Navin reached out and gave Sunjoy a bear hug and said, "Don't worry, yaar. Let me handle this. I'll come up with a solution."

Sunjoy calmed down a bit. Navin would always do as he said.

Navin sat silent for a few minutes. Then he lit up. "Of course! It's the only way. Let's offer the girl the second lead in your next film. She will be happy to even be a lamp post in an A-list project."

"But..." Sunjoy began to protest but lapsed into silence. He tugged at his shirt sleeves – something he was wont to do when nervous – as he thought hard. This did not sound good. Sunjoy had an extremely nervous temperament and though he was not superstitious, he had always feared the evil eye. Things had been going swimmingly well for him so far. As they said in the business, his *tarakki was din doguni raat chauguni* and his partnership with Navin was the talk of the town. He always worried that the dream run could come to a crashing end someday. He hoped it wasn't happening now.

Navin sensed Sunjoy's thoughts and said, "Don't worry about the role, yaar. The second heroine will have a minuscule part really. I have the perfect script. I've been working on it for a few years by myself. I wanted to direct it as my own next film. But now the situation demands that you take the reins. It's a full hero-led macho-actioner. *Naam se hi hit hai* ... *Gully Gangs*. What do you say?"

Sunjoy nodded meekly.

"Ok, let me speak to her and sort it out."

Navin immediately called a number putting the caller on speaker phone.

"Surabhi, my favourite girl. How are you? Now listen, forget all the *party-sharty mein yeh-hua woh-hua* stuff. *Yeh sab to hota hi rahta hai.* Sunjoy is otherwise a gem of a man. He's the best person I know in this world to launch you and he will. In fact, we just discussed the perfect project for you which will be announced soon."

The voice on the other side sounded excited, but also hesitant. Navin told her that he would personally discuss the details with her and take care of everything. She would meet Sunjoy only on the sets. After almost half an hour of smooth, sugary assurances, Navin hung up with something of a satisfied smile.

"What a piece of work these youngsters are. After landing a part in a big film, now she wants a fee increase over and above what we have signed her for. Anyway, beggars can't be choosers," grumbled Navin.

Then looking at Sunjoy's dejected face he said, "Cheer up, yaar. We have nipped this problem in the bud so let's celebrate. *Party-sharty karte hain*. At my place this evening."

Sunjoy looked relieved but also a little unhappy. He nodded.

"Eight-thirty p.m. sharp and then we can do an all-nighter and tweak the script for this girl. Just like the good old times," said Navin before he left as abruptly and dramatically as he had come in.

*

That evening Sunjoy fetched up with a strained look on his face as he sat in his car, a gleaming panther black BMW X7.

Ram who sat next to him was wondering if it was because of what had happened in the conference room between Sunjoy and Navin. *It is funny to see your boss getting fired by his ex-boss*, thought Ram. He felt a little sorry for Sunjoy. *My boss really is too Bhola Bhala*.

"Please don't drink tonight, sir," whispered Ram, with an anxious smile.

"Pass me the cigarette," Sunjoy said gruffly, as he reached out to borrow Ram's pack. To Ram, this was the ultimate sign that Sunjoy was nervous.

When they got to Navin's plush sea-facing bungalow Sunjoy continued looking grim. Ram had an inkling that there was some trouble in paradise and he was even more worried than usual as he would certainly have to face the music the morning after, no matter that none of it was his fault.

The well-appointed lift, designed like those period lifts from the British era, took them straight to the terrace. Navin's wife, Priya, greeted Sunjoy with a smile as they alighted.

"Why didn't you get Renu?" she asked, always the perfect hostess.

Sunjoy just shrugged and remained silent. He wasn't in the mood for pleasantries. He headed straight to the bar and started with a large glass of the choicest whiskey.

Navin was at the far end of the terrace surrounded by his team who were a constant fixture at his parties. A few select friends of Navin and Priya were trickling in. Navin excused himself saying, "I'll just go and show my face to the guests. Sunjoy, why don't you come along to tell them something of our new project?"

Sunjoy nodded and then on second thoughts asked Navin to go ahead and do the talking. "I'll join in at the time of the formal announcement," he said moodily.

After Navin left, Sunjoy took Ram aside and asked, "Is Surabhi here too?"

Ram nodded.

"I want to chat with her. Can you ask her to meet me by the fountain at the lower level of the terrace garden?"

Ram raised a quizzical eyebrow but nodded again and left to accomplish his mission.

Sunjoy hung back in the company of Navin's team members. This seemed more fun than making polite conversation with strangers. There was Abbas, Kabir and Vijay. Abbas and Kabir, like him, were cinematographers with plans to turn to direction. While Vijay was Navin's favourite go-to music director, singer and lyricist.

They hugged Sunjoy one by one, congratulating him for yet another film with Navin.

"I've got to admit, though … we thought that after you announced your own banner, we'd be finally rid of you. But it's almost magical how you two always find a way to get back together," said Kabir, laughing.

Out of the corner of his eye, Sunjoy saw Ram heading back towards them. Ram gave Sunjoy the thumbs up. Sunjoy casually sauntered away from the group and walked up to Surabhi who was standing by the fountain. He started chatting with her as if nothing had ever happened. Surabhi was a little hesitant at first, but Sunjoy laid on the charm and soon she was giggling profusely at his jokes and asides. Sunjoy then said, "You know, Surabhi, I really liked the audition that you'd done for the webseries Navin is producing. I felt that maybe I could reach out to you for the main lead in a film I'm doing under my own banner. But I guess I screwed things up by getting drunk and doing something terrible that I would never dream of otherwise. I really apologise for my regrettable actions. Anyway, as things turn out, we *are* going to work together. I'm excited about that and just wanted to let you know that you have nothing to worry about."

"Wow! Sir, you really think I'm that good?" she asked.

Sunjoy nodded. "Yes. You are a natural."

Surabhi was overcome by emotion. She suddenly dived and touched Sunjoy's feet and then as she rose whispered something in his ear.

The music was very loud so Ram, who was lingering nearby, keeping an eye on Sunjoy, could not figure what Surabhi was saying.

As the night wore on, Sunjoy got more and more sloshed much to Ram's consternation. He adored Sunjoy for his intelligence and kindness too. Even to a greenhorn like Ram, it was evident that his boss was something of a creative genius, too caught up in his world of stories and fascinating characters to notice the machinations of the real world. Ram worried about Sunjoy's naivete and genuine nature. It just wouldn't do if his boss ever looked like a loser. It would not reflect well on Ram who took his duties as an assistant to India's leading director very seriously. The morning-after gossip among assistants and those bloody blind items could kill Sunjoy's carefully earned image and in turn damage Ram's prospects too.

He slid next to Sunjoy and tried to coax him into eating. "Sir, this chicken kebab is to die for." And before Sunjoy could refuse, he had a meaty morsel almost thrust down his throat by the ever-vigilant and attentive Ram!

Once Ram felt he had suitably fed and distracted Sunjoy, he steered him towards where the action was – to the table where Navin and Priya were seated along with their hangers-on. A mock arm-wrestling match was going on. Sunjoy, quite evidently in a happy mood after the copious amounts of spirits he had consumed, threw the gauntlet at Navin and said, "*Navin bhai, ho jai ek round*?"

Navin joined in the merriment without batting an eyelid and beat Sunjoy within a few minutes.

"Why do you even try when you know you'll never win," Navin guffawed during the ceremonial hug between the victor and vanquished.

Much to Navin's surprise, instead of throwing back a sheepish repartee, Sunjoy grew emotional.

"It's true Navin-bhai. I can never win. I am such a useless loser. I always let alcohol get the better of me. You got me to start off on my own feet and I shot myself in the foot with my drunken behaviour."

Sunjoy blabbered on and turned to Priya, "Bhabhiji, do you know how much he trusted me? And I let him down."

Navin and Priya tried to pacify him but he just would not listen. Before they knew it, Sunjoy burst into tears.

The team had started collecting around them. Nothing makes colleagues happier than seeing the star of the team make an ass of himself at a party.

By now Sunjoy was on his knees with folded hands. "Sir, I am sooo drunk. I was drunk like this only when you told me to stand guard outside Maya's vanity while you two made out. I really deserve to be punished." Navin tried to hush him, but Sunjoy only turned louder. "Bhabhiji, please forgive me that despite my loyalty to your husband, I could not save him from the disgrace when Maya's fiancée walked in on them and gave Navin-bhai a black eye!"

Priya looked on dumbfounded. Navin almost screamed, "*Oye, bevde, tu kya bakwas kar raha ha*!"

Sunjoy continued unperturbed.

"I don't deserve a second chance. Once I was so drunk on a shoot that I forgot to tell you to not come to pick him up. You arrived just as he was leaving with Maya in his car. I had to throw myself in front of your car and pretend to be hurt. You took me to the hospital and tended to me so lovingly. I'm sorry to do that to you."

By now Navin looked like he could kill Sunjoy.

Navin shouted at his manager Bunty to bundle up Sunjoy and put him in the car. Bunty tugged at Sunjoy's arm, but Sunjoy paid him no mind.

"Navin-bhai, you are my guru. You have given me one more chance. I won't let you down anymore. I promise. Priya Bhabhi, I'm sorry. Please forgive me."

In the dim lights, Navin glanced at Priya. Only he could read the expression on her face. Finally, he looked away, his eyes downcast.

Priya turned to Sunjoy. "No, Sunjoy. I'm afraid that won't be possible. Navin won't ever work with you again."

As he got into the car and headed home with Ram by his side, Sunjoy snapped out of his stupor as though he'd never been drunk. He sank into the comfortable seats of his car, smiled to himself and said, "Finally, I'm a free bird."

Ram looked at him in wonder. "So it was all an act?"

Sunjoy smiled mischievously. "Is that what you think?"

Ram nodded, then asked, "What did Surabhi tell you?"

"She confirmed my suspicions. Nothing happened between us. The day after the party, it was Navin who asked her to send that message to him. He told her that she'd get a part in my next film if he could pressure me into it. When Surabhi realised that I wanted to work with her anyway, and that she was missing out on a really plum role under my banner, she decided to switch sides and come clean."

Ram looked at his boss with renewed admiration, thinking, *Hey Bhagwaan, thank you! Director Bhola Bhala is not so Bhola after all!*

Love Bungalow

"I entered the bungalow, and went towards Daler's study. As you know, there is an old mirror in the corridor that reflects a corner of the study. And, suddenly, to my utter surprise, I caught a fleeting glimpse of a movement through the corner of my eye. *Mujhe aisa laga* that there was a girl with Daler, a foreigner with blonde hair…"

Nimmi Bajwa, a buxom lady in her sixties, attired in a peach-and-cream kurta and cigarette pants, was once again regaling her friends with a new anecdote, recounting each detail with the finesse of a seasoned raconteur. As usual, all her close friends had put away their phones and leaned forward to get the details. A dramatic pause here, the drop of her voice to a conspiratorial whisper there, was how she had reeled them all in.

Mrs Bajwa's stories, sprinkled with a generous dose of mirch-masala, always livened up the gathering and she never disappointed when hosting a soiree at her well-appointed British-style bungalow. She plied her guests with a variety of delicacies, and wine and cocktails, and often it was tough to tell which of Mrs Bajwa's offerings was the bigger draw – her amusing stories dripping with gossip and narrated with as much drama as a movie, or her generous table.

Of course, it followed but naturally that in most of these stories, it was Mrs Bajwa playing the central protagonist – a desired beauty, a mortified martyr, the perfect mother, and most often, the most fortunate and blessed woman in their tight-knit group. The lady's audience, however, kept coming back for more despite the predictable nature of her discourse, perhaps for some of the aforementioned reasons.

Presently she was in the middle of an anecdote to highlight the virtues, loyalty in particular, of her famous husband Daler Bajwa. An unkind cut in a roomful of ladies who knew otherwise about their better halves, you'd say. Or even risky. But, nothing could stop Mrs Bajwa once she started.

"Yes. A foreigner girl with blonde hair. I was numb with shock for a few seconds. I rushed to the door. I knocked and Daler opened the door after a couple of minutes. He was looking sleepy, as if he'd been taking a nap. I barged into the room without a word and started looking around. The desk was fine, but the cushions on the sofa were a little topsy-turvy. I looked around, checked inside the loo and even crawled below the desk. At my age it is nearly impossible, but I was so overcome by anger that I managed even that." She paused for half a beat.

"*Phir*?" prompted Mrs Shah eagerly.

"*Arrey phir kya tha*? Daler looked stunned. He kept asking me, 'What's the matter?' I looked everywhere but there was no girl. There was no one in the room, but Daler. Suddenly, I realised that I had conjured something up in my mind. It was as if I was drunk or had consumed what these young kids nowadays have … Ecstasy or something. It was so embarrassing. But, thankfully, Daler was understanding. He sat me down, got me some water and then let me rest through the day. The next day, he even got me a beautiful antique gold set … temple style … as an early Diwali gift. And he booked us for a luxurious London holiday. My sweet, sweet Daler … did not mention another word of the incident. He put it down to my blood pressure and hormones. I felt so terrible about the whole thing. How could I have doubted him after being married for thirty-five years! Daler really is such a wonderful hubby … so unlike the typical filmi men. You all know exactly the kind of men I'm taking about, na…"

Everyone nodded in agreement. "Yes, Nimmi, you are lucky to have a husband like that," said one of them. Everyone exuded mock sighs, feigning envy while in reality they were merely being sympathetic. Really, there was nothing worse than being proven wrong in a situation like this. It was certainly better to be proven right despite facing the humiliating confirmation of being cheated on. Because then, one had a bargaining chip to reboot and renegotiate the terms of the relationship. But a miscalculation such as this meant eating humble pie. And worse, having to remain mum over any future transgression. The only silver lining in all of this for the woman was the generous gift from her husband.

"You are so foolish … even if there was a girl, you should know that Bajwa is not going anywhere, not at this age, well past his prime. Now you will never hear the end of it," said Mrs Suri, an old and dear friend of Mrs Bajwa's. She never shied away from meting out tough advice.

Mrs Bajwa's fair face paled further. "I know. I should have waited it out before jumping the gun. Anyway, it turned out to be my imagination," she said, looking miserable. On being reminded by one of her acolytes about her husband's generous gifts, she found her spirits lifted considerably. God had been kind. Or at least her husband had been. God bless him.

Lost in her thoughts, Mrs Suri sipped her cocktail and reached out for one of the delicious shrimp starters. Something did not add up for her. Daler Bajwa was not a man who would let something like this pass and reward his wife for doubting him. No way. He was as chauvinistic as they come. Mrs Suri had known Nimmi since college. They had been so excited when they came to know that she was marrying an upcoming actor who had played a villain in many films. Back then Daler was a strapping young man, and so good looking. But there were rumours that he had quite a roving eye. Oddly enough, Nimmi Bajwa's feminine instincts had remained oblivious to all of her husband's transgressions through their younger years. Daler Bajwa had somehow managed to steer clear of any scandals.

Serendipitously, after Nimmi and Daler got married, his career took an upturn. Even though he played the villain, he started getting meaty roles. A couple of hits later he was dubbed a legit star who specialised in negative roles. The Bajwas celebrated their good fortune by shifting from their older, spacious yet modest premises at Breach Candy to their current sprawling bungalow many moons ago. Daler was at the height of his career working triple shifts in far-flung studios around Goregaon and Powai. Bandra was just the right place to be where the stalwarts of Hindi cinema resided. It was crystal clear in Daler Bajwa's mind that his wife Nimmi had come into his life as something of a good-luck charm. One that he could not lose. It was for this reason too that he took utmost care to be discreet about his affairs. And Nooristan, the bungalow Daler had managed to snap up, was an exciting story by itself. It had proved lucky too.

After three consecutive golden jubilees, he was rolling in money. It was whispered that he was getting paid as much as the heroes! People came in droves to watch Daler Bajwa in a film. As the story went, producer Lalwani, who had bankrolled some of his biggest films like *Kagaz*, *Patjhar* and so on, always said, "More people want to watch Daler Bajwa saying his dialogues and terrifying them before dying at the hands of the hero than watching Devinder Sharma and Upamanyu Kumar sing romantic songs with their heroines!"

It was quite true. A hush would fall in cinema halls when Daler made his entry with a panther-like quiet menace.

He would always have great lines. *Is thand ke mausam mein itna paseena*? was one such signature dialogue. He would deliver all his lines with a trademark sneer that would send a chill down many a spine. And the crowd would go into raptures waiting for the hero's rebuttal.

Outside of the movies, Daler was no less adventurous. He loved a great lifestyle – cigars, choicest whiskeys, fancy cars, you name it. His most cherished dream of course was to live in a sprawling homestead just like Jagdish Kumar's Nooristan bungalow on Pali Hill. Lady Luck smiled once again at Daler Bajwa. Precisely at that juncture, Jagdish Kumar himself passed away and his famed bungalow went up for sale. Luckily for Daler, Jagdish Kumar's children had moved to Canada and he had outlived his dear wife by a decade. His fortunes were on the downswing at the time of his death and the circumstances around his death had been suspicious. There were whispers of a burglary. An inside job, no doubt gone wrong, resulting in his death, which was quite possibly a murder. But there was never any concrete proof. Just rumours swirling around. It was all too unsavoury for his genteel family who wanted to put the tragedy behind them and move on. They put Nooristan up for sale.

But Daler was not the only one eyeing Nooristan. Devinder Sharma, the veteran comedy hero, too longed for this legendary home and perhaps Upamanyu Kumar would have thrown his hat in the ring too if he didn't already have his sprawling property in the area. Nooristan held a strange fascination for these men. And the way they vied to possess it almost mirrored their desperate efforts to outdo each other in front of the leading ladies they were wooing. The beautiful bungalow – with wide gates opening into a driveway shaded by a canopy of beautiful gulmohar trees that lead to the main house with its gorgeous balustrade holding a small balcony at the entrance– was enchanting to say the very least. There were a few bigger and more picturesque bungalows in the vicinity, but none that were desired by the most powerful men in showbusiness. The excitement once the house was declared to be on the block was unprecedented and it soon became the talk of the town.

As far as everyone knew the deal had been done with Devinder but there was a certain amount of money that remained to be paid. Devinder was counting on a big cash payout from a producer but somehow the money didn't turn up in time. The producer was also a great friend of Daler's and owed him one. Daler didn't skip a beat in nixing

Devinder's deal by borrowing a grand sum from his friend so that he had to defer Devinder's payment.

Then he approached Jagdish Kumar's family, first extending his condolences and then expressing his desire to live in a house just like Jagdish-ji's.

Jagdish Kumar's son promptly asked him, "So why don't you?"

Daler couldn't believe his ears. He had never imagined that his ploy to put forward his intentions at such a delicate moment would land in the right spot. Daler grabbed the bungalow deal right from under Devinder's nose.

Nooristan proved even more lucky for Daler Bajwa. His career continued to shine. Shortly after moving in, he even landed some prominent supporting roles in Hollywood films much to everyone's surprise. It dawned on the curious bunch that it was possibly the 'Good Luck' factor that made Nooristan the most desired property on the block.

Nobody except close friends of the family like Mrs Suri knew about the unimaginable lengths Daler would go to, to get his luck going. He had wangled an invite from one of his star buddies when Hollywood hotshot director Tony Alamo was in town. He'd heard that one of Alamo's productions required a senior actor to play a Pakistani immigrant in London. It was a small part but Daler wanted to beat his heroes once again and get to international glory before they could.

At the party, not only did he get an introduction with the famous Alamo, but also convinced the Hollywood honcho that he had no trouble personally ushering him around Dharavi and other pockets which formed the underbelly of the city. That is how Daler had landed a role that became the launchpad for many of his roles in Hollywood. Daler's stock had risen way beyond any of his contemporaries. After all, for us Indians what better validation than a stamp of approval from the West!

Now, this whole incident about Daler in his study brought back those memories. Mrs Suri had not forgotten those early rumours about Daler's proclivities. She made up her mind to get to the bottom of this suspicious event. After all, Nimmi had diligently kept tabs on Mrs Suri's late husband, a producer, whenever Mrs Suri would be away at her parents to look after them. She made a mental note to talk to her son on the matter and find out if there could be any truth to it. She was good at playing a snoop and would not think twice about it if it could help her friend.

Mrs Suri's son, Bicky, was an actor himself. He was familiar with Daler Bajwa's circle. It would be easy to find out if the old rascal had got himself a new young squeeze. Mrs Suri liked nothing better than gossip about industry geezers. But this once, she suffered a pang of guilt as it involved her dear friend.

At her family dinner that night, Mrs Suri buttonholed Bicky. Being the astute woman she was, she knew better than to approach things head-on with her son. She went about it in a roundabout manner that she felt would arouse her son's interest and get his attention.

"Bicky Beta, do you know these days there are all these Russian women around in the industry. I have heard they are really desperate, latching on to these senior actors and directors … is that true?

Bicky didn't bat an eyelid. He knew his mother's ways. She was fishing for something. He decided to play along till she came out with it. "Yes, Mummy, you know how these foreigners keep coming in droves – they all feel that Bollywood is the best place for them. And if they are slim and young, they do get picked up as dancers. But why are you suddenly interested in them?"

"Arrey beta, I heard that our Daler has picked up someone like that. When his wife was about to catch him red-handed in his study, the girl just vanished into thin air! Now the poor wife has to live with the guilt and anxiety. Horrible for the poor woman, if you ask me." Mrs Suri shuddered rather dramatically befitting her position as an actor's mother and fixed an enquiring look on her son.

Bicky was expressionless, but smiled inwardly. He was familiar with the wicked ways of the industry men. That old fox Daler Bajwa was surely up to having a few flings with firangis. In fact, Bicky had pulled off some crazy stunts himself. But, even if it was his mother asking, it was the bro-code to not land another man in trouble.

"Mom, it is possible that Nimmi Aunty just imagined it, you know. Sometimes your mind leads you to these crazy thoughts and hallucinations if you are insecure or something. Which she certainly must be, given Daler uncle's reputation and the fact that she is not a celebrity like him."

His mother gave him a cold stare. "Enough of your pop-psychology, Bicky. I am sure you know something. Out with it now. Or I will tell your girlfriend Shipra about that other one who dropped in at three a.m. to meet you," she said.

Bicky was furious with his mom for spying on him.

The perils of staying under one roof with your parents! he thought to himself. Realising that the best way out was to not say anything at all, he continued to eat his meal silently.

Mrs Suri, however, was unrelenting. "Bicky Beta, if Daler is all that I've heard about him, I don't know if he's ever going to mend his ways. You know what they say … leopards don't change their spots overnight!"

Bicky didn't even nod in agreement at this. Mrs Suri realised that she had to appeal to him in another way. She made her most *bechari-face* and said, "Beta, you know Daler's son-in-law Shiven. Please promise me that you'll have a discreet word with him and tell him to get his father-in-law to back off from his philandering. I don't want Nimmi to go through anything crazy at this age."

Bicky knew that the only way he could get his mother off his back was to do as she said. This last request offered a way out for him. "Okay, Mom, I'll get the message across to Shiven and let's see what he says."

*

A few days later, Bicky invited Shiven for a boy's night out at his club.

Over a lavish dinner and drinks the two began sharing the latest industry gossip and then Bicky brought up the delicate topic of Daler Bajwa's mysterious peccadillo.

"Bro, promise you are not going to say this to anyone because it involves your family," Bicky whispered conspiratorially.

"Oh! Cross my heart. There's nothing I like more than family secrets," replied Shiven with a mischievous smile.

"It's about Daler Uncle."

"Even better. It's always good to know about the skeletons in your father-in-law's closet."

Bicky lowered his voice further. "I have known this for some years. I never thought that I'll speak about it. But, I guess the time has come."

"Bro, enough suspense. Tell me, yaar."

"Okay … okay … You see … Many years back … after that legendary incident in the eighties, when Daler Uncle was once almost caught on the set … how should I say … in-flagrante-delicto with a young actress, he decided that he had to think of a better way to continue with his escapades. He did not want his lucky mascot Nimmi Aunty to find out and leave him. Plus he was not getting younger. It was around the time that the bungalow of Jagdish Kumar was on the block. It was expensive but Daler Uncle bought it, working multiple shifts like a dog. Why do you think he'd do that?"

Shiven looked puzzled. "Of course! That stuff is no secret! I know the whole story of the tricks with which he pipped others to clinch the deal."

"Yes. But why do you think he wanted it so bad?"

"Well it was the superstar Jagdish Kumar's house. So obviously it was a matter of great prestige for someone like Pa … Daler Bajwa, who was something of an upstart at that time, to come in and swoop the deal. It was his way of saying to the world that he was as good as the heroes of the day. To gain a greater social legitimacy I suppose," Shiven said.

"Hmm. Yes. All of that. But there was more. Well, you see, Daler Uncle had been to Nooristan for a party when Jagdish Kumar owned it. There he was among some old Bombay moneymen who were trading old stories. The story that caught his attention was that Nooristan had once belonged to a Pathan merchant who was involved in smuggling activities during the British Raj. Nooristan apparently had a big secret passage leading to the outer garden. The merchant had built this to escape the British soldiers if he was ever raided. And the old men at that party were joking about how Jagdish Uncle could use it to smuggle in his mistresses without his wife knowing! That information stayed with Daler Uncle. And the minute the bungalow was on the block, he fought tooth-and-nail to buy the place."

"But how do you know all this?" Shiven asked Bicky.

"Because Daler Uncle told me about it once when we were shooting together in a similar old Parsi bungalow in Khandala. He was drunk and blurted out the whole story," said Bicky, lowering his voice again.

An awkward silence followed and then finally Shiven said, "So why are you telling me all this?"

"Bro, my mom was worried about your mother-in-law. Nimmi Aunty spotted a firang in the house who suddenly disappeared. The minute my mother told me this I knew what had happened. So, I'm just telling you to get the message across to your father-in-law to cool it."

"Why can't you tell him directly? After all, you're the one with whom he shared the secret of Nooristan," said Shiven.

Bicky sighed. "Yaar, we are working together in a film soon and I don't want things to get awkward. But the bigger problem is that if I tell him, he will give Nimmi Aunty hell for sharing the anecdote with her friends. And if I don't do 'something about it' as instructed by Mother, she will not hesitate turning into Momzilla and spilling some secrets of mine."

"Yeah. I understand your mom does like to share your family's dirty laundry in public. Man! She's going to give you hell! But how can I speak about this to Daler Pa-ji? He is my father-in-law."

"Think of something, bro. I leave it to you."

In the days that followed, Shiven racked his brains thinking about all the different ways in which he could bring up the subject with his father-in-law to get out of the sticky situation. He even considered discussing it with his wife. Maybe she could issue the warning to the old man but then, his father-in-law could well point out that it was a case of the pot calling the kettle black.

What a terrible subject to broach with any man, least of all your father-in-law, when he does have some idea that you are sowing your wild oats as well. But then again he often says that do unto others as you would like them to do unto you. Maybe I should try that route and see if that sort of gets the message across. This could turn out to be fun. Shiven chuckled to himself.

*

Days passed. One day, as Bicky came down to the family dinner he saw that his mom was looking very stressed.

"What happened, Ma. Everything okay?" he asked.

"*Kya bataoon*, beta, today I met Nimmi and her daughter

Reshma. Both were very anxious and restless. I asked them if all was well. And Nimmi said, 'Arrey, what to say. We were doing fine. But recently Reshma thought she saw a girl in her father's study with Shiven. She went to check. There was no one. Now Shiven is young and not forgiving like my husband. He has been very upset and has refused to come home till Reshma apologises and promises to never suspect him again. I don't know how this could be happening. Is there some kind of ghost of a young girl. *Koi dayaan ghar mein ghus gayi hai kya*?'"

It took Bicky all his training and experience as an actor to keep a straight face.

With a dramatic swing of the hand to her forehead, Mrs Suri continued, "*Main ki karaan*? I told Nimmi that a good long havan is the only way to keep away these negative influences. What do you think, Bicky Beta?"

Bicky rolled his eyes heavenwards, cursed Shiven under his breath, and said, "Haan. That sounds like a good idea. That should take care of all ghosts, imaginary or otherwise."

Meray Paas Maa Hai

Arjun Saxena woke up to a perfect mid-morning with the sun blazing over the Arabian Sea outside the large French windows of his bedroom. The sky, with a splash of perfect white clouds across a bright blue background, resembled a film poster. His grey cat curled up at his feet purred happily while the air was fragrant with the smell of coffee being brewed. Arjun rolled out of bed and peeped out through the windows. As usual, a noisy crowd was clamouring outside his terraced bungalow. It was 11 a.m. already and seeing the restless crowd outside his home was reassuring. Things could not get better. He loved crowds mobbing his residence or his car.

It was after the first show of his film *Love Match* that he got his first taste of the intoxicating allure of crowds. He had stepped outside the gates of Gaiety Theatre in Bandra after the first-day-first-show. The buoyant, houseful crowd in the theatre had been quite exhilarating, but it was the response outside that made him giddy. Arjun suddenly observed people staring and pointing to him. And in a jiffy, they were all around him excitedly shouting his name, asking for autographs.

"*Le, ab tu star bann gaya,*" said his mother, who had accompanied him, as she raised her folded hands to the heavens to thank the Movie Gods. "Remember this moment and always aim to keep them happy," his mother had added for good measure.

Arjun smiled to himself at the memory. He had been a somewhat introverted child, so in the beginning it annoyed the hell out of him to have complete strangers touch him and pull at his clothes in hysteria. But, over the years he had begun to enjoy it. He even smiled at the few cheeky onlookers who, when they finally got a glimpse of the 'star', would walk away disappointed saying, "He looks so unimpressive!"

In fact, he occasionally encouraged cheeky comebacks from fans because it spiced things up a bit. Unquestioning adulation was great for the business, but engagement, by which his fans became his thinking conscience keepers, was even better. He found being "Mr Nice" all the time tiresome. Sure, it worked well for him on several fronts, but it was tough to live up to the expectations 24x7. Like the other day he was smoking on his terrace and a photo of the same made it to the gossip sites, stirring a debate on whether role models should conduct themselves more responsibly.

That was another Arjun Saxena quirk – stirring up things just that little bit to keep himself in the news cycle. Showbusiness, Arjun had realized, was all about grabbing attention, seizing the moment, gauging the mood and telling almost the same story in multiple ways. And he was very good with that too.

But as of now his mind was preoccupied with planning the next phase of his career. He had a brave new film coming up and he could take no chances. This had to be a hit too to complete the hat-trick of hits. The last two films had been super-duper blockbusters and he was keen to hit the ball out of the park with his third which could both impress the critics as well as be a money spinner. With a hat-trick in the bag, a star could survive years of flops. He planned to PR the hell out of it and create such a halo that marketers and advertisers would keep throwing endorsements at his feet for years to come.

"Juice, please!" he hollered to Manu Kaka, his old faithful who went scurrying to do the needful. One of the perks of being an actor, a superstar actually, was that things were always getting done for you. You didn't have to lift a finger. Not unless the director was shouting action!

When Manu Kaka returned with his glass of fresh kale juice, he mentioned that Naresh, Arjun's ex-security manager, had called. He was in the neighbourhood and wanted to introduce a friend to Arjun.

Arjun was immediately wary. Naresh had served Arjun well, but a kidney problem had forced him to retire. He had an annoying habit of boasting about his starry connection and would bring all sorts of oddballs to meet Arjun. Arjun knew that Naresh was probably extracting favours or even money from the 'friends' he brought along to meet Arjun. He had not been in touch with Arjun for over a year. And Arjun was in no mood for a meeting with Naresh. He had too much going on to waste time on Naresh and his friend.

"Tell him, I am not at home," Arjun shot back at Manu Kaka.

Manu Kaka stopped dead in his tracks and shot Arjun a reproachful look. Manu had been with him for the longest and he derived some strange pleasure when he saw 'Saab' meeting regular people of his rank. It probably gave him a sense of dignity about his station in life. Manu Kaka's look had the desired effect. Arjun was suitably guilt-tripped.

Arjun shrugged. "Oh … all right. Tell him I will be on my way to the gym in fifteen minutes. If he can make it by then…"

Arjun's big problem at this time was that his wife Ragini and he were in the middle of another spat. She'd found out about his silly little fling with a pretty young dance choreographer. Arjun had cast himself in the old mould, where keeping up appearances was important. To the general public he was a happily married superstar, loyal, loving and so on. He was not half of it. But he firmly believed in the mantra that there's no harm pretending if it made you popular.

He needed to sort things out with Ragini before things got out of hand. He didn't want any bad PR about his personal life taking away the focus from his new film. Or his countless brand endorsements slipping away with bad publicity.

He had tried all the usual methods of appeasement. He had got her a beautiful Van Cleef & Arpels set. But, Ragini knew him only too well and had seen through his guilt-edged gifts. "I can't be happy with fancy cars or an expensive jewellery set … I need respect and honesty," she'd said as she left to spend a few days at the Juhu apartment they maintained as a private guesthouse.

Women! Here I am spending precious time trying to mend matters with my wife while I should be focusing on promoting my film, he thought to himself as he went about changing his T-shirt to get ready for the gym. *This waste of mind-space is certainly not going to help my cause.*

"I am going to the gym, Manu Kaka. I will meet Naresh some other time," he called out. But, as he walked into his living room he saw that Naresh was seated there with a beefy-looking, balding, middle-aged man who was reeking of cheap perfume.

"*Arrey, Naresh, kaisa hai tu? Kabhi aaya?*" Arjun asked, surprised at the promptness with which Naresh had landed up.

"I was down at the gates … Manu said you are on your way to the gym. Why don't we come along. That way we won't hold you up."

Reluctant at first, Arjun paused and considered the idea for a second. It sounded far better than having some random guy hanging around in his home.

Within minutes they were in the car. Naresh sat with Arjun in the back seat of the spacious gleaming Bentley while the beefy stranger who had been waiting patiently without a word sat in the front.

A quick introduction later, the stranger, whose name was Hamid, spoke up. His soft voice belied his build. "We are all huge fans of yours, Arjun-ji," he said.

Arjun beamed with folded hands and mouthed his standard line, "It's all His grace and the love of people like you." This he said while rolling down the windows to blow away the smell of Hamid's perfume which was getting on his nerves. He knew that the man wanted something. Arjun thought it best to get down to it right away. "Tell me, what can I do for you?"

"Arjun-ji, *woh aisa hai ki main Bhai ke taraf se aaya hoon.* He wants to meet you."

Arjun nodded distractedly. There was no doubt that Naresh was getting some money from Hamid for this. He turned to Naresh. "Why not! Please call Hamid and his brother to our next premiere."

Naresh nodded but his face was expressionless.

Hamid spoke again, "Actually, Arjun-ji, *Bhai ki beti aapki bahut badi fan hai.* She is getting married next week and … She loves that song of yours … you know … '*O meri soulmate, kar le mujhe date*' …"

Arjun was a little annoyed. Hamid was turning out to be a real pest. But, Arjun maintained an even tone and did not let his irritation show.

"I am a little busy with the promotions of my new film. I won't have the time to attend the wedding. But do bring her to the premiere and I will meet her there," Arjun replied.

Hamid didn't react to what Arjun had just said. Instead, he said, "She wants to dance with you at her wedding."

Arjun was appalled at the temerity of Hamid's demands. He turned to Naresh. "Naresh, does this man know what he is saying. Has he any idea who I am?"

Naresh didn't say a word, instead he lowered his face and scrutinized the dark tinted car window with great interest.

Hamid was silent for a few seconds, then he quietly said, "Arjun-ji, I know that you are early for your gym today. Yesterday you had gone at 12.30, the day-before at 2. Yesterday, you took your Porsche and were wearing a blue t-shirt and black striped track pant. *Aur haan … aapne Asics ke gym shoes pehne thay.*"

Arjun was now shocked. He glanced at Naresh. But Naresh was still expressionless, his eyes downcast.

Before he could say anything, Hamid spoke again. His tone was still respectful. "Arjun-ji, *main Bada Chetan ka aadmi hoon*. He is like a brother to me. That's why he sent me personally to invite you. You see, he can't come … he stays in Dubai, you know."

For a minute Arjun was close to panicking. The Bhai Hamid was talking about was Chetan Nambiar alias Bada Chetan, the dreaded Mumbai gangster who gained infamy operating from Dharavi, but now lived in Dubai. People said that he had gone legit, but from time to time there were whispers of how he had extorted huge payoffs from builders, industrialists and film honchos. Those who went against him had been shot at as a warning. Needless to say, no one dared to oppose him. The police had been helpless as he had the top brass from both countries in his pocket.

Arjun gulped, wondering how to end the conversation with Hamid. Beating up baddies on screen was one thing but handling them in life was a different ballgame altogether. And he sucked at it. He flashed a murderous glare at Naresh. Naresh kept looking at the tinted-glass window with laser-focus intensity. Arjun realized that Naresh too was under pressure otherwise he would never have brought Hamid to him. Anyway, Naresh's mission had been accomplished. He had delivered on his promise to Hamid. Now he could hope to be left in peace by his gang of trigger-happy shooters.

Arjun quickly decided that false bravado or any sort of glibness would work against him. So he opted for a meek,

Bheegi Billi avatar which his sidekicks would play in a movie. "Hamid-bhai, I am a little busy these days. Let me think and get back," Arjun said as politely as he could.

Hamid said, "We are well aware of your schedule, Arjun-ji. It's just that Bhai is busy too but he always makes time for two things … the requests of his friends … and taking special care of those who are not his friends. We will wait for your call." Then, turning to the driver abruptly, he said, the menace in his voice apparent, "*Gaadi rok.*"

The driver stopped the car. A shining silver Mercedes appeared in front of Arjun's car. Hamid nodded to Arjun and slid out. Naresh followed suit. They stepped towards the Mercedes, opened the door and sat inside. The Mercedes took off. Only after the Mercedes had disappeared into the traffic did Arjun tell his driver to resume their journey.

The seriousness of the situation finally sunk in. Arjun's heart began to hammer in his chest. He began to sweat profusely, and his mouth went dry. He looked out of the car to make sure the silver Mercedes was out of sight. His head was reeling but he realized that he was near the Santa Cruz Lion's Club Garden. Was he having an anxiety attack, or worse, a heart attack, he wondered. There was only one place he could go. "The Juhu flat … *jaldi,*" he barked at the driver and then sank back into the seat.

*

Arjun opened his eyes and saw Ragini looking down at him. The worry lines on her face creased her radiant skin.

"Are you feeling okay now, Arjun?"

He tried to get up but he was feeling a little woozy. Ragini helped him sit up and propped a cushion behind him. He realized he had been lying on the large sofa in the living room of the Juhu flat.

"You came in looking like you'd swallowed a *khatta* lime whole. You vomited on the floor and crashed on the couch. What happened? Drank too much at your little whore's flat last night?"

"Ragini, please I am not in the mood for your caustic remarks right now. So, if you could just spare me the insult. I am in a bit of a jam."

'Okay, okay … I was just wondering. After all that girl…"

"Forget all that bullshit about the girl. That's long over and it meant nothing anyway. I need your help now."

Ragini was Arjun's childhood sweetheart, their love story had been a part of every magazine feature on love. But, more importantly she had always been Arjun's friend, philosopher and guide through all the years. Over time he'd probably fallen out of love with her, but she'd always been his rock.

He needed her now more than ever, but first he needed to get some things sorted between them so that they didn't have problems like their current ones again.

"Look. I understand I haven't been the perfect husband, but I have always taken good care of you … except for the odd *occasional* affair," he said with a stress on 'occasional'.

She rolled her eyes but didn't interrupt.

"If it wasn't for that, we could both agree that it's been a good run. I know for a fact that you've also had a couple of brief affairs. Before you start denying them, I'd like to say that I understand. We've always been friends first and then lovers. So why don't we continue as friends, remain husband and wife to the world and carry out our indiscretions discreetly? It's a win-win. I can put it down as an agreement. If you continue with the arrangement of being my wife, you get a regular monthly stipend more than the alimony you'll ever get if we divorce. Besides that, this flat and expenses of all your staff plus your exotic European holidays will also be taken care of. We can even throw in an occasional roll in the sheets with me if you like?"

Ragini didn't protest. Instead she asked, "And what happens if you suddenly decide to marry a twenty-year-old like the one you are presently fooling around with?"

"Ah, now I knew you could ask me that, so here's the thing. If it ever comes to that, though it won't because you are the only woman I have ever loved, the terms of this arrangement will not change. I owe you that. I will get it done by my lawyer and it will all be run past you." Arjun had really thought this through. It was a price totally worth paying for his cherished stardom.

"I am sure this offer is not coming from just the goodness of your heart!" Ragini shot back. For once, she had the upper hand instead of the superstar husband, always being so entitled and self-righteous, even when he was lying through his teeth about his affairs.

"Come on..." Arjun protested weakly and then decided to drop it.

He sank back into the sofa looking extremely stressed.

For a fleeting moment, just like the old times, Ragini felt sorry for him. If only they could go back in time. But she had learnt not to be a sentimental fool anymore.

"Okay, out with it. What's eating you?"

Arjun was almost glad that Ragini was with him in this stressful moment. He never had to be guarded with her even though she gave him a hard time unlike the women he had been dating.

"Actually, that dreaded gangster Bada Chetan has sent me a message that he wants me to dance at his daughter's wedding in Dubai," Arjun replied haltingly.

"What! Are you crazy! Nowadays no one gets involved with gangsters. Think of what will happen if the media finds out. Your fans will chew you up on Twitter."

"Don't I know that? Bada Chetan's men have been following me. His man Hamid, who made his way into my car, brushed off my 'I'm very busy' excuse with suggestive advice on not messing around with Bhai's invitations! How do I say no to them? I can't call the cops because Bada Chetan will come to know and it will become even more dangerous. What should I do to make sure this blows over?"

"Fuck! Yes, this is a tricky situation."

Ragini lapsed into silence. Arjun let her be. Ragini's mind was obviously going over each and every possible scenario. Arjun hoped she would come up with something helpful.

He had built his stardom with so much passion and hard work. Being a superstar was not as easy as it looked from the other side. It was hard work maintaining an image. And now this Bhai wanted to meet him and ruin his image! This could not have come at a worse time.

Now he really knew what his mother had meant when she had warned a young brash Arjun about what being anointed a star meant. His mother, an English teacher in a local Mumbai school, always knocked sense in his head.

She would tell him, "Remember, uneasy lies the head…"

"That wears the crown," he would complete the sentence.

He fiddled with his phone and dialled his mother's number. "Hi, Mom, how're you doing?" he asked, taking care to bring in a breeziness into his voice. His mother of course could always tell when he was troubled.

Thankfully his mother was cooking and was distracted. "Just preparing the prasad for the puja I am doing for the success of your film."

"Thanks, Mom, you work too hard; you should have asked the cook. You will tire yourself out unnecessarily."

"Yes, nowadays I do feel a little tired. Maybe I need a holiday. Just a short one, not too many days. I don't want to waste too much money."

Arjun smiled. It was just like his mom to not be wasteful. She was a strict and disciplined person. A no-nonsense stickler for a simple, minimalistic life.

"Don't worry, Mom, we'll go for a holiday after the film is released."

"Okay, beta, now you get back to work. I'll go and finish my cooking."

"Bye, Mom, love you," said Arjun as he disconnected.

He looked towards Ragini. She had a curious look in her eyes.

"What? You know the daily updates that I have with my mom," he uttered by way of explanation.

"Yeah, of course I do … But while you were doing your ladla beta thing, I was doing some Googling on Bada Chetan and guess what? I just got an idea that could get you out of this mess."

"What is it?" Arjun sat up excitedly.

Ragini was getting impatient. "Arrey, my husband-with-benefits, here it is..." She showed him her phone screen with a random Mother's Day tweet from Bada Chetan. In it, Bada Chetan had thanked his late Ma for always protecting him from harm by sending him blessings from her place in the heavens.

"Mister Arjun Saxena, you are going on that holiday you just promised your mother, before you meet the big Bhai..." said Ragini, laughing with abandon.

"What! Why?" asked Arjun, cursing Ragini under his breath for trying to spoil his secret trip planned with a young actress. And then suddenly the penny dropped. Ragini was not messing up his amorous plans, she had an idea to extricate him from the Bhai mess that he was in.

"*Achcha*!" he said. "*Kuchh idea aaya, Madam-ji*! Tell me na!"

Ragini smiled mysteriously.

"But wait ... It's benefit time first!" said Arjun, smiling mischievously in return.

He got up and scooped her into his arms and took her into the bedroom.

*

Later as they lay in bed, satiated, Arjun dialled a number.

It was Gaurav Santania's personal mobile. Gaurav was the CEO of Hi-Tek Electronics. Arjun was the brand ambassador for all of Hi-Tek's products from mobiles to refrigerators. The call was picked up after the first ring itself. A loud

American-accented voice boomed at him, "Arjun bro, to what do I owe the pleasure of your call?"

Arjun purred in his sexy starry voice, "Amazing job you are doing at Hi-Tek, yaar. What marketing! Truly blown away by your genius, Gaurav." Arjun laid on the flattery thick when it came to moneymen. Like all stars he never let his vanity come in the way of making big bucks. Unlike stars from the older generation, he understood that corporate heads and other men-in-suits were gatekeepers to generous funds. The sky was truly the limit for stars like Arjun if they kept corporate honchos happy.

"Bro, you're talking about us winning the sponsorship of the inaugural Interworld-Gulf Cricket League, right? Yes, it is great news, yaar. It's very last moment and all, but the American sponsor had some issues and dropped out. And we've stepped in. Huge opportunity for us!"

Arjun was charm personified. "Achha, I know the inaugural match is being held in Dubai next week. I'd like to start the proceedings for Hi-Tek. Why don't you speak to the cricket association to let me do the symbolic toss for the first game?"

This was followed by raucous laughter at Gaurav's end, and then an excited query, "Bro, I thought you were busy with youı film. Will you really be able make time for it?"

"Of course, bro. Anything to make this deal the most special one for Hi-Tek. I am the brand ambassador after all." In any case, Arjun knew he would make a few more crores from the appearance.

Gaurav couldn't control his excitement. "I'm on it. Consider it done."

"Super! My manager will be in touch with your executives to work out the financial and other arrangements."

"Absolutely, bro. See you in Dubai!" said Gaurav as Arjun disconnected.

Immediately after, he called his mother, "Mom, next week, you and I are going for a short holiday."

*

The crowd roared with excitement. The inaugural match of the Interworld-Gulf Cricket League deserved no less. The Heartland Hit Man, Pallav Pandit, was living up to his title and smashing the ball at will. He was clearly a crowd favourite in Dubai. He had just hit the ball to the stands and the cheerleaders had got into their act.

Hi-Tek mobile phone ads played on the multiple screens and the cameras panned to Arjun in the special VVIP box. He waved out and blew kisses at his fans when the camera panned onto him. Seated next to Arjun was his mother, visibly excited at watching a cricket match with her favourite player in action. Arjun pointed out to his mother that she was on the big screen and asked her to blow a kiss at the camera. Annoyed at being interrupted, his mother shot him an angry look. "Don't behave like a silly boy, Arjun."

Unknown to Arjun, the cameras could also pick up the directional sound. The crowd heard what Arjun's mother said to him and burst into collective laughter. Arjun's face grew red with embarrassment. Never one to lose his presence of mind in front of the camera he gave a sheepish smile and shrugged at the cameras as his mother continued being engrossed in the game, ignoring him.

Arjun turned his attention away from his mother and began to look around at all the other hi-powered attendees in the VVIP box. His eyes rested on a big, moustachioed man seated at the far end of the very same VVIP box. This was Bada Chetan. Bhai may have been declared a dubious figure in India but offshores, he fronted a respectable real estate business and there was nothing odd about him being present at the match. He was known to be a cricket lover.

Arjun was about to look away, but now Bada Chetan was looking at him. Arjun smiled and folded his hands in a namaste. Then he got up from his seat and nonchalantly walked towards the F&B stand. He was ordering a drink when out of the corner of his eyes he saw Bada Chetan get up and walk towards the bar. Arjun picked up his glass and turned. Bada Chetan was now in front of him. Arjun smiled and raised his glass. Bada Chetan smiled and gave him the thumbs up as he said, "Arjun Bhai, we finally meet. My daughter is very excited that you will be at her wedding day after tomorrow."

Arjun smiled politely as he said, "Chetan Bhai, I'm glad that I can tell you this in person so that you know it's the truth. You just saw my mother make mincemeat out of me so you can tell that nothing in my life moves without her permission."

Bada Chetan nodded. "Yes, mothers are special. I have a lot of respect for mothers," he said haltingly.

Arjun took a deep breath and said, "So … this is how things stand, Chetan Bhai. I won't be able to come to the wedding. I asked my mother and she absolutely forbids it. She doesn't like what you do."

"B-but, what's it got to do with my *dhanda*? This is about my daughter's wedding."

"I know that, Chetan Bhai, but try explaining that to my mother. Nor can I go against her wishes."

"*Magar*..."

"You have already seen how angry she can get..." Arjun said with a sincerity that would have convinced anyone. "But if you want to find out for yourself, she is sitting out there," he added, looking in his mother's direction nervously.

Bada Chetan looked stumped. Providentially, at that very moment there was a replay of the exchange between Arjun and his mother on the giant screen, her irritated admonishment of Arjun on public display, loud and clear, followed by Arjun's goofy embarrassment.

Arjun's mother turned towards the bar looking for Arjun. Bada Chetan saw her looking in their direction and he folded hands in a namaste from a distance.

Bada Chetan turned towards Arjun. He stared into Arjun's eyes. Arjun held his gaze unflinchingly.

Bada Chetan didn't say anything for almost a minute. Just when the tension was getting unbearable for Arjun, Bada Chetan broke the silence and said, "I understand your situation, Arjun Bhai. And I respect your mother's decision. I too wouldn't have gone against my mother's wishes. Even if my life was under threat."

Arjun held his breath.

After a pause that felt like a lifetime to Arjun, Bada Chetan shrugged. "Don't worry. There is no threat from me to you. A man who respects his mother should be respected himself. This has been my life's belief."

Bada Chetan turned and walked out from the box without another word.

"It worked!" Arjun wanted to shout out but concealed his emotions well.

Ragini's idea had paid off. If there was anyone in the world Bada Chetan respected unfailingly, it was his own mother and those of others too. Knowing this, Ragini had bet that Bada Chetan would buy into Arjun's excuse of not going against his mother's wishes. More importantly, Bada Chetan had an understanding of maternal temperaments and quirks. The video exchange between the mother and son that Arjun had engineered had been the clincher. Bada Chetan had a reputation to protect. He knew better than to dent his fear-inducing image by getting a public dressing down from an old lady. He was old-school that way.

Arjun's mother smiled at him as he approached. "You seem to be back in a good mood. Who was the man you were with over there? Looked like a decent guy. Very respectful. Why didn't you bring him here?"

With an angelic smile, Arjun held his ears and said, "Ah! Mom. You can be very stern and intimidating sometimes. But, scary or strict, I guess I'm lucky that… *meray paas Maa hai.*"

Papa Kehte Hain

Tufts of cloud flocked around the chartered six-seater Cessna 206 parting the azure sky in two infinite halves. Inside, Simran, on her way back from the holy Ajmer Sharif dargah, was sitting by the window with her hands clasped in a prayer. *The sky is the best place to send out additional prayers to Bhagwaanji.* And this occasion required serious intervention. Simran's new film, *Good Luck*, was about to release. After a dud last year, this film was critical to her career. And, there was an even bigger challenge on the horizon. Acclaimed Hollywood director Raymond Woods was in town to scout for a Bollywood heroine for his next film in the famous action franchise 'KickBlast'. To outwit her rivals and be the first of her generation to crossover and star in an International A-list film, Simran knew she had to play her cards well.

Simran never thought any dream was too big for her. The confidence stemmed not from her enviable good looks, talent or mastery of craft; it was because she was blessed a little more than others. After all, she had the yesteryears star Mahesh Khanna for a father, her one-of-a-kind superstar 'Papa'.

*

A gaggle of paparazzi broke through the security barricades at the airport and a series of cameras sprung to life as Simran stepped out of the airport. The young star remained unfazed. Fame had been a constant companion ever since she was born. Anticipating the photographers, she had taken care to touch up the concealer and her lipstick. *Nothing too over the top; just a dab of pink lipstick and mascara.* Simran smiled at the paparazzi, feigning surprise. Although she desperately wanted to call Reema, her publicist, to find out the reactions at the *Good Luck* sneak preview that morning, Simran posed graciously for the photographers. The screening, which had been organized for a select group of senior editors, would have just ended.

Simran knew she was very good in the film. It was an author-backed role and Papa had deliberately opted for Manish Vyas, the director who was known more as an auteur than as a masala film-maker. This way, she would get the lion's share of the credit and if things went south, as they often did at the box-office, the blame would rest with the director. *Thank god for Papa. He thought of everything.*

*

Once she was safely ensconced in her Jaguar, Simran didn't wait to catch her breath. Instead, she dialled Reema on her diamante-studded iPhone. Reema Verma was a seasoned film publicist famous for her aggressive and often controversial publicity of her film star clients. Reema loved to boast that while others stayed in the news, her clients always made headlines. Her oft-quoted line was one borrowed from

American showman Phineas T. Barnum. "There is no such thing as bad publicity."

After a great deal of difficulty, Simran had convinced Papa to sign up with Reema. As a father who was extremely protective of his only child, Mahesh Khanna was a little wary of controversies, but his resistance had eventually caved in. Given the serendipitous series of events, Simran's choice appeared to have been a smart one.

"Babes, you are the *bestest*, thanks for that great welcome," Simran purred into the phone.

Matching her client's excitement, Reema gushed with equal fervour from the other side, "Darling, where are you? They are all dying to meet you."

"They are? That's great news." Simran wanted to rush to the screening room, but Papa's voice echoed in her ears, "*Make them wait a little or they will walk all over you.*"

"Reema, let them wait a little considering how mean they have been with my last film. Tell them I will be there shortly." Before Reema could say anything further, Simran cut the line.

As her car glided on the western express highway, Simran started scrolling down the messages flashing on her phone.

Everyone, practically everyone at the screening, was sending in flattering compliments. There were plenty accompanied by emojis of hugs and claps, which was a good sign. It was particularly reassuring that Yogesh Mehta, considered a Bollywood trade-shark, had predicted a good future at the box-office for *Good Luck*. Gita Mehra, critic at *The India Tribune*, had assured her of a 4-star rating which was huge because it was the biggest news daily in India. The critics, after almost three years of disapproval, had changed their tune. For a moment Simran forgave them for their earlier barbed comments and concentrated on relishing her success. It had come after a long wait.

"*Simran displays a control over her craft that is masterful.*"

"*Good luck is brilliant film-making with all departments in perfect sync with each other. The performance by leading lady Simran Khanna is impeccable.*"

"*A memorable performance by Simran Khanna.*"

These were just a few of the headlines she saw in her mind's eye.

Papa's famous dialogue from his hit film *Suraj Ka Samrat* flashed in her head. *Chadhte suraj ke saamne sab sar jhukate hain.*

That montage of glorious and congratulatory headlines Simran was conjuring was rudely interrupted by a thought bubble of a rather contradictory nature.

Take that Divya Rao, you fucking small-town wannabe! You think you can ever top an Industry Kid?

*

Divya Rao had burst on the scene two years after Simran, to a rousing reception from the media. Surprisingly, even the otherwise cautious and guarded film fraternity had warmed up to the new girl almost instantly. This middle-class, Plain Jane from Nagpur was unlike the glamorous Miss India's that Simran thought to be her real competitors. According to Simran, she looked like a *ghisi-piti* girl-next-door and dressed like a *behenji*. Papa had predicted that Divya's career would be short-lived. According to him, Divya's worst disqualification was that she was overeducated. Papa had warned Simran, "*Nobody likes a Miss Know-It-All on the sets of a film. It is one thing to be educated, quite another to show-off to the director your knowledge of screenplay writing. You'll only piss off the male co-stars and directors who are the real power centre in the industry.*"

But Divya Rao had proved to be a smart cookie. After her first hit, she had landed many additional zeroes on her cheque for acting opposite south Indian superstar Vijaywardhan in a Tamil film. Given her newfound success and his own desperate quest for a hit, the leading man had convinced the producer to accept Divya's unreasonable demands. The resounding success of the film had emboldened her. With a series of canny choices, especially projects that other heroines considered too risky, she had pretty much cornered the market. Divya's last film *Tinder Love*, a romantic comedy, had worked its magic with both the audience and the critics. All the A-list male stars and directors were falling over each other to work with her.

Simran hated the fact that she was at a great disadvantage when it came to taking on someone like Divya. *These middle-class girls who're not industry kids have it easy. No expectations, no lineage to live up to.* Unlike Simran, who had to abide by a "no-kissing and no intimate scenes" rule set by Papa, Divya's love for smoking up and occasionally hooking up with her directors had worked to her advantage. Simran had made sure that the rumour mills about Divya's peccadillos kept churning. But, meanwhile she had missed out many A-list projects because of her restrictions.

That is until her last film that had turned out to be a dud at the box-office. Finally, Papa had given her a little leeway to experiment, and she had picked out the screenplay for the slightly arty *Good Luck*. Under Papa's watchful eye, *Good Luck* had turned into a middle-of-the-road *commercialish* multiplex film about a young feisty woman who changes the fortunes of her entire village by educating and freeing them of the clutches of the exploitative village sarpanch.

Unfortunately, Divya Rao too had a film releasing the same week. Given her popularity with the media, who thought she was the next best thing after sliced bread, Divya was sure to get great press that weekend. Simran would have hated it if her career-best performance lost out to Divya's mediocre talent.

Her phone rang, bringing Simran out of here reverie. It was Reema, calling to inform her that the photographers had dutifully lined up to capture her arrival at the preview.

After a pitstop at home, the Jaguar circled back to the Flame Preview Theatre.

Before stepping out, she checked her make-up – *skin looking natural and flawless, check*; *hair curls gathered in a soft updo, check*; *a loose strand skimming my bare shoulder, check.* She had made it a point to change into a denim jumpsuit for a working-class look. Simran looked like the very picture of congeniality. *Perfect attire to make this moment perfect.* Simran prided herself for being perceptive.

A synchronised wave of flashing light blubs blinded her as she stepped out in the dark parking lot.

Simran feigned surprise again at the sight of the lined photographers.

Reema rushed towards her with the urgency of a security chief guarding a visiting head of state.

Beaming that perfect endearing smile that she had practised several times over with Reema in order to make her look approachable, Simran stepped into a sea of compliments.

While she flashed a friendly and charming smile, Simran made a mental note of all those who were absent.

*

"Divya, your film has hit the bullseye! Mohan Pathak and other trade analysts are predicting it to be not just a hit but a blockbuster," shouted Ramesh Sagar, Divya's manager. He sighed under his breath. Managing Ms Smarty Pants, who had the highest expectations from those who worked for her, was a tough job.

In her sea-facing terrace apartment on Carter Road, Divya, her lithe frame bathed in the golden sunlight, turned to him with a steely look. She knew better than to be fooled by Ramesh-ji's silly prattle.

"I have got all of five messages from any of the reviewers or reporters. I did see a few tweets that have called the film a one-time watch but not a word about my acting abilities or the stunts I performed. Or about all the effort that went into losing ten kilos for the role!" Divya's voice had risen considerably over the civilized decibels that she normally maintained. Right now, her screams were loud enough for Ramesh-ji to wonder how a woman who barely had a twenty-inch waist could have such ferocity in her voice. Her fair, heart-shaped face framed by cascading locks was an angry red, one solitary vein on her neck throbbing and bobbing with the exertion.

Ramesh-ji knew it was time to calm her down before she went crazy. He had an inkling about what may have brought about this outburst. Gingerly, he rolled her a fat spliff, and with a sense of urgency handed it to her.

"This film will not only be the biggest hit of your career, it will be the biggest hit of ALL times," he said, gesticulating with his arms, hoping the emphasis on the word 'all' would calm her.

Divya puffed at the doobie, staring angrily at him through the smokescreen. She was far from pacified. Apart from the lukewarm response to her film, the unending tweets declaring Simran Khanna's performance in *Good Luck* as one of the finest that year had irked her no end.

Nobody was going to focus on the big bucks that Divya's film would rake in. The entire credit for its success would be handed over to Vikram, the hero of the film who had practically sleepwalked through it. The audience, however, loved his swag so much that the theatre would erupt the minute he walked into the frame.

The media was so fucking fickle! They had abandoned her just when she needed good word of mouth for her performance. It was critical to her plans of wooing Raymond Woods. The fact that it was Simran Khanna they were rooting for pissed her off even more. Divya knew Simran to be quite the Juhu memsahib always looking down her nose at colleagues without a filmi pedigree because she did not find them classy enough. Ironically, when it came to sneaky low-lying activities, Little Miss Khanna was leagues ahead of all the other Bollywood leading ladies. But Divya was too smart and had figured very early that Simran was using her papa's clout to try and dissuade important producers from casting Divya in their projects. Luckily the producers didn't really care for anything other than money; and Divya's films made money. So, they cast her again and again.

Divya was a confident self-made girl. Unfortunately, success had turned her head. Like several of her tribe, she had over time grown accustomed to believing that her mere presence was a favour for the media. However, this time around things had been different. The unexpected media-swing towards Simran Khanna had shaken her up. Simran, guided by her Papa's *industrywala* instincts and of course, a lengthy, well-thought-out PR campaign way before her film's release, had won this round. Divya had begun to sense a shift in her fortunes.

Divya did not have a publicist. Ramesh-ji was her Man Friday for all bad press exigencies, but he was quite obviously incapable of keeping the media on her side.

"Why did we not organize a screening for senior editors?" she asked him impatiently.

"Madam, there was no need. The production house had organized a press show for them," said Ramesh-ji.

"You should have kept in touch with people on my behalf and sent the important media people Diwali gifts etcetera while I was away shooting for my films … Isn't that your job?" Divya was shouting again.

Ramesh-ji didn't give a direct reply. He knew better than to argue with her on such matters. "Do not worry, madam. We will wait for the weekend to be over and I am confident that the film will not only hold, it will grow."

Divya let Ramesh-ji finish and then abruptly requested him to leave her alone. Puzzled and relieved in equal measure, he left.

Divya sank into the white leather sofa, staring impassively at the sun setting into the Arabian Sea in the distance.

A short while later she picked up her mobile and scrolled through the contacts, searching for a number. When she found it, she dialled it immediately. When the call was picked up at the other end, Divya spoke out before the other party could even say hello, "Babes, how are you? No time for your friends these days? Congratulations on the big success of *Good Luck*. I know this was not possible without you. Come and have a coffee with me, na ... like right now types," Divya cooed to Reema over the phone.

When the need arose, Divya could charm the birds off the trees. It was her special talent, which she used every time she found herself in a tight spot. Like just now! She knew she had Reema curious and interested.

*

Reema could not stop smiling like a Cheshire Cat. She knew what that call meant. Finally, she would have the distinction of handling publicity for two top actresses and arch-rivals to boot. The campaign she had been running for Simran Khanna had borne fruit. It had started with a complete overhaul of the reportage around Miss Khanna. First, she put out stories about her acting classes in NYU. It was a bit of a stretch but not a complete lie. Simran did go for a trial class to test it for her younger cousin who was to be enrolled. Next, fashion shoots were put on hold and she had made it clear to all fashion magazine editors that Simran could not do photo-shoots because her contract forbade her from disclosing the look she had in *Good Luck*. Then Reema began to plant information indicating that Simran was someone who took her craft seriously. The media bought into the ruse without any questions. Simran too had warmed up to the task. She had slipped into her new image of a method actor with surprising ease. Besides fashion, Simran had the knack of speaking with amazing authority on subjects she knew least about. Her switch from talking about Louis Vuitton to Roberto Fellini had been swift. And the best part was that she made it all look so natural and seamless.

Publicity these days was not so hard except that you had to pay a packet for coverage in the leading papers. But then again Simran's papa was ready to pay for beti's publicity.

Unlike Ms Rao who thought she was too big a star to pay for being interviewed. *Now she gets it!*

About a year ago, Divya had dismissed Reema's pitch for her PR campaign, which involved spending big bucks for publicity. But now the shoe was on the other foot. Divya had reached out to her instead. Reema had been in the business long enough to smell desperation from far away. She liked desperation. It paid her bills and put the designer threads in her wardrobe. Yes, signs of desperation were her favourite emotions in a film star.

Taking her own sweet time, Reema made her way to Divya's glitzy apartment. *Ms Rao does have the Midas touch*, she ceded grudgingly, walking into a lobby that resembled a five-star hotel. There was a separate lift for the penthouse with a staff member to chaperone her. Doing the mental math in her head, she knew she could ask Divya for a fee of at least Rs 50 to 60 lakh; the money that she needed desperately for paying her staff a bonus and getting herself a nice holiday in Greece. Simran and her papa were a good mention on Reema's CV but in money terms, the remuneration sucked. These *industrywalas* were real skinflints, always reluctant to part with their money when it came to people who worked for them.

Ramesh-ji, who was hovering in the meeting room at the lower level of the duplex apartment, eyed Reema suspiciously but he had no choice but to let her through. He decided it was best to join hands with the competitor till he was back in Divya's good books. The frown on his face turned into a benevolent smile. Expecting Reema's arrival, Divya called on the intercom to instruct Ramesh-ji to send her upstairs.

In Divya's private chamber, the girls met like long-lost friends.

"You have just lost so much weight, Reema. Giving us heroines a run for our money, haan?" Divya trilled.

The two sat and chatted for hours, recalling the days when both were struggling to make ends meet in Mumbai.

"Remember that one time when we were sharing a chicken sandwich and coffee at Barista because we were so broke? Back then I predicted that you'd be at the top," Reema said.

Divya smiled and proceeded authoritatively. "Babes, you have to work on my next project but exclusively. You have done your bit for the little Miss Muffet. Now it's high time you moved up in life."

Reema's shoulders loosened. She was relieved to see that things were on track.

"Actually, I'm quite happy with the way things are working out with Simran and her papa, Mr Khanna. I..."

Divya butted in. "I don't know about that, yaar ... you have worked so hard for the Khannas ... why aren't they paying you?"

Reema hesitated. Divya had obviously done her homework.

Reema's phone started buzzing. It was Simran. She raised the phone and showed the name flashing on the screen to Divya. Then with a smile and an exaggerated gesture she put the phone on silent and slipped it into her bag without answering it. Reema had been waiting hand on foot on Simran for the last six months, she didn't mind making her wait a little. Right now, she needed to secure the bounty she had come for.

"Well, to tell you the truth, I did what I did for Simran because she and her papa are like family to me. But I could sure do with a little extra ... paycheck wise."

Divya had been waiting for this moment. Looking Reema straight in the eye, Divya played her trump card. "I believe you've got a special meeting lined up with Raymond Woods and his agent tonight. Surely, it's about the Bollywood actress who'll play the lead in his next film in the 'KickBlast' franchise?"

Reema was startled. How did Divya know that she had set up an exclusive chat for the Khannas at the party that night at the Taj Mahal Hotel. Covering her surprise with a disarming smile, she shot back. "I don't know, yaar ... whether these Hollywood films are a good idea for you.

They don't have any good parts for Bollywood heroines. Plus, I don't like arranging all this auditioning for the part bit because stars like you don't like screen-testing for roles. You know that."

Before she could continue, Divya cut in again. "As they say in Hollywood, let me make you an offer that you cannot refuse. I will pay you one crore rupees as your fee … provided you sign a contract as my exclusive publicist and manager. No other stars on your client list for the next two years, starting now. And I want you to swing the Hollywood deal in my favour. I will pay you an additional 15 per cent of my fee on that project. But you have fifteen minutes to decide."

Divya got up and walked out of the room, leaving Reema open-mouthed.

*

Simran, exhausted with her lengthy interaction with the media, wanted to rush home. Late afternoon was usually time she spent with Yazmin, her personal trainer who ensured that Simran stayed in good shape. Otherwise slender, Simran had hips with a tendency to flare out disproportionately at the slightest provocation. And her love for Indian cuisine didn't help. Her nutritionist had been smart. She had formulated a plan where Simran had to eat every two hours so that she did not binge. In fact, at this time, Simran was supposed to have finished off the carefully prepared meal of grilled fish with just a touch of lemon butter sauce, sautéed vegetables and a very small portion of brown rice. She wanted to disappear somewhere and just have her meal.

She was puzzled by Reema's behaviour. Tonight was her big opportunity to remind Simran of her invaluable service and she had just walked away quietly with a broad smile suggesting that Simran spend some quality time with the journalists, especially those from leading newspapers and websites. One of the junior members of her team had stayed back to watch over the proceedings while Reema had bounced out of the theatre.

As her hunger pangs grew, Simran's smile began to droop and her replies were now reduced to bare necessities. She was just getting ready to leave when Lily Motwani, the witch Papa hated, and who was famous for her widely read snide columns in *Hello Bollywood*, rushed in. Lily looked a little out of breath but she reached out to air-kiss and embrace Simran.

"Darling, tell me it's not true that you slept with Manish Vyas for the role in *Good Luck*. I'd like to simply believe that you have talent!" Lily hissed in Simran's ears.

Simran froze.

Within an instant, her face turned red and she was screaming her lungs out at Lily. In a fit of rage, she tried to move the clinging Lily away from her but not realising her own strength, she ended up pushing her hard. Lily Motwani fell back on a chair next to them with a shocked expression while everyone else looked on horrified. A photographer accompanying the scribe quickly clicked a photograph of the fallen Lily who held the pose just long enough to be framed as a tragic victim, before walking out. It all happened in a flash. Everybody else averted their gaze, pretending as though they had not seen anything happen.

Simran, who was too stunned to even react, just rushed to her car and it drove her away. *Papa knows the owner of* Hello Bollywood. *He'll ensure that they don't run a story.* But Simran knew that the Internet whisperers would carry the tales of her public misdemeanour far and wide. Her big fear was that the whispers would reach Raymond Woods's ears. *Where is Reema when I need her? She needs a talking to.* She dialled her father's number and blurted out what had transpired. He spoke to her in his soothing voice. To her surprise, he already knew that something would go wrong soon. One of his close friends had spotted Reema sipping a Cosmopolitan at the Marriott with the devil woman Lily just half an hour ago. Papa had already put two and two together.

Simran was aghast. She couldn't believe what Papa was hinting at. Papa then forbade her from going to the party that night saying, "Don't worry about Raymond Woods. Let me handle it, beta."

Simran put down the phone. She couldn't ignore the sinking feeling in her stomach. Her thoughts stirred her to a near frenzy. She could feel a migraine attack coming on. Soon she threw up on the expensive pure leather seat of her car. She was certainly in no condition to meet Raymond Woods.

*

The party in the Crystal Room at Taj Mahal Hotel was buzzing with high-powered glamour. The who's who of Bollywood was present. The buzz doing the rounds was that Simran Khanna had decided to skip the event, given that the media had boycotted her. Reema made her way to Divya who was chatting excitedly with Andrew Barton, Raymond Woods's agent. Reema had ensured they met earlier. When Barton excused himself to fetch Divya a drink, Reema raised a quizzical eyebrow.

"So, how's it going?"

"Great! He's coming back with drinks and then ushering me to Raymond Woods," replied Divya.

Reema gave her a wink and the 'thumbs up' and turned to leave. As she stepped away, Divya called out to her, "By the way, that incident with Simran and Lily was … spectacular."

It was Reema's turn to flash a cheeky smile. "I aim to please."

Just then Reema caught sight of Mahesh Khanna across the room. He had cornered Raymond Woods and had struck up a conversation with him. Reema looked on helplessly. This could mean the end of her dream and Divya's as well. Simran's papa, she knew, was quite the shark. Suddenly, Reema caught his eye. Tossing her a triumphant smile, he looked away, resuming his conversation with Woods who seemed to be quite interested in what Khanna was saying. Reema's heart sank to her knees.

*

Simran was seated in her father's plush study waiting for him to fill her in on the details of the previous night's party. Hopefully the reports of her mishap with Lily had not reached Raymond Woods. Although with all the bad press that she had received across social media, even someone living under the rock would have heard of the incident. She sighed. She needed a miracle and her Ajmer Sharif wish had already been used up. *Good Luck* had been successful. *Did one visit grant two wishes?* She was yet to find out.

Feeling the need to distract herself, she reached out for a book and then remembered that all books in the cabinet were hollow spines. Papa was not much for reading. He considered it a waste of time.

How did things go so horribly wrong? Why did I react so angrily to Lily Motwani's question?

Everyone knew it was not true.

That cow used the oldest trick in the book and riled me.

Simran was restless. How much longer would Papa make her wait? She reached for her phone and went to Twitter and soon found how Papa had 'handled' her problem!

Twitter was aflutter with news that Divya Rao was the chosen one for the Hollywood project *KickBlast-9*.

Simran felt crushed. Tears of frustration and defeat began to well up in her eyes. Just then Papa walked into the study.

"Congratulations, beta," he said with a smile.

Holding back her tears, she looked at him with irritation. "What congratulations! That bitch Divya has been signed for the Hollywood film, not me," she whined.

"Yes, but Divya will be in Los Angeles for a whole year, and guess who's going to rule Bollywood while Divya's away," said Papa.

Simran stared at him nonplussed.

Papa pointed at the iPad in his hands.

The headline in the entertainment sections of the online news sites read SIMRAN KHANNA TOPS CELEB SENSEX AMONG ACTRESSES. And then the strap: "Signs up four A-list projects with top Bollywood producers overnight."

Papa had been busy at the party. He broke into his beatific smile. "I 'strongly' recommended Divya to Woods last night. The fool congratulated me on my sporting spirit and my gracious honesty."

A hint of a smile began to appear at the edges of Simran's lips as it slowly began to sink in.

"By the time she's back you'll cement your place as the undisputed No. 1. No Hollywood-shollywood returned will be able to shake your position."

Simran's face lit up with a big smile.

Like in Bollywood films, Papa had saved the day and made sure there was a happy ending.

Pyar, PR Aur Purana Chawal

"Bye, Somesh sir. It was such an honour catching up with you. I am really looking forward to this opportunity of a lifetime," trilled the young star Rishabh Sippy as he traipsed out of the impressive swan-shaped doors of Hansa Productions, the production house which belonged to erstwhile hotshot film producer Somesh Hanswani.

Seated alone in his massive cabin, on a throne-like chair, in front of a wall displaying somewhat faded posters and photographs of the hit films under his banner, Somesh Hanswani heaved a sigh of relief. His heart was still pumping with excitement. It was after a long time that a young star had said 'yes' to working with him. Sending up a thank you to the Big Guy in the sky, Somesh switched on some meditative chants on his music system and sat still, breathing in and out. He let his mind reflect over recent events.

The casting for Somesh's new project which intended to put Hansa Productions back on the Bollywood map was turning out to be a lot more difficult than Somesh had anticipated.

Before Rishabh, he had discreetly sent out feelers to three A-list superstars but hadn't found any purchase. Rishabh, to his mind, was a bit of a comedown. But, Somesh had reconciled, thinking that that someone from the list of top five or six stars was good enough. He generally tended to be more in favour of traditional casting choices of the regular industry *familywalas*. Rishabh was an outsider. He was, however, the new flavour of the season with the young and restless audiences. Plus his fee was flexible, a very attractive feature for studios and financiers. Also, Somesh's old-favourite – director Akash Darpan – would come on board only if Hansa Productions managed to rope in Rishabh.

Much to Somesh's embarrassment, Rishabh had given him quite the run-around. Rishabh knew that he was Somesh's fourth choice and had made it a point to underline that he was not so easy to get. He wasn't going to let go the insult of not being the first choice so easily. Somesh's offer and Hansa Productions' flagging fortunes had given him the golden opportunity to avenge this slight.

But, Somesh being the player that he was had wined, dined and cajoled Rishabh over a period of a couple of weeks and ultimately convinced him to say yes to Hansa Productions' next film. Now, as Somesh meditated, he couldn't help marvelling inwardly at his own charisma and his power to convince people.

After spending a few minutes in a reflective state, Somesh reached a state of equilibrium. He was now ready to get on with the day. He turned off the chants and buzzed his secretary for a few quick updates and to fix up meetings with the film-studio honchos. Somesh then jumped into a meeting with Akash Darpan whom he had called for the new film. As he went about setting things up during the rest of the day, Somesh could not get himself to stop smiling. Yes, he was back and on a roll.

*

At 6 p.m., Somesh dialled the man who was to bankroll his next film, Gyan Chandwani, the diamond merchant.

"Chandwani-ji, how are you? You won't believe what good news I have for you. We can finally take our project forward. I think I have just the perfect hero for the film … the young Rishabh Sippy. I had a meeting with him and he sounded very excited so maybe you should meet him too."

"Hmm…" Chandwani's voice on the other end of the line sounded unimpressed. "Are you sure about him?"

"Oh yes, Rishabh is a very talented boy. And, you know how well his last film has done. It was a blockbuster."

"No, I meant, are you sure about Rishabh agreeing to your project? Because I just saw his tweet where he has grandly announced that he is now only working with new-age producers and that he just rejected a big offer from your production house. I quote him, 'No longer play safe. Want to do something different. Take a walk on the wild side. Do cutting-edge stuff, something my heart says I should.'"

"What!" Somesh felt as if he had been kicked in the gut. He disconnected, making an excuse, and quickly checked Twitter. And sure enough there was the devastating statement which was now trending news on Rishabh's fan-club Twitter handle with the hashtags- #rishabh #walkonthewildside.

Somesh had not expected this sudden and inexplicable volte-face. Why had Rishabh agreed to do a simple safe love story with Somesh when he really wanted to do something edgy? Somesh could have offered him something offbeat too. Yes, that's what he would do. He would offer Rishabh a carte blanche to do whatever he wanted under his banner.

His mind made up, Somesh dialled Rishabh. But the phone just rang and rang. Somesh knew there was only one way he could force Rishabh's hand now. He dialled his friend Mohan, who was Rishabh's cousin, and had brokered the meeting between them. But Mohan's phone too kept ringing. Somesh knew what these unattended calls meant. It was the filmi way of saying 'No' or 'Sorry, can't do'. The Bollywood brush-off.

Dejected, he slumped back in his majestic throne-chair. Forlornly holding his head in his hands, Somesh sat still, wondering what to do next. A while later, he got a message from Rishabh. Somesh's heart skipped a beat in excitement. But it was short-lived. Rishabh was suggesting a replacement for himself – Mandar Singh, a second-rung star known better for his biceps and glutes than acting chops.

Somesh gritted his teeth. Rishabh's message was the ultimate insult to Somesh whose family had been in this business for almost fifty years. Once upon a time, people would give their right arm and the shirts off their backs to work with him and now even a Johnny-come-lately was giving him the heave-ho! "Ah! This treacherous world of showbusiness," he muttered to himself.

By the next morning, Somesh's worst fears had come true. Rishabh's rejection was followed by Chandwani backing off and then Akash Darpan dropping out of the project apparently due to a sudden family tragedy! The writing was on the wall and in the newspapers. Rishabh Sippy Exits Somesh Hanswani's Film. Hansa Productions' Revival Seems Doomed, announced the morning headlines.

Somesh racked his brains hard trying desperately to figure out what he needed to do to protect his flailing film business. Apparently, he, Somesh Hanswani, had lost out his advantage of having an established old film production banner thanks to the arrival of these new, cool, edgy film-makers and producers whom the new corporate studio heads now respected and loved.

After further rumination, Somesh decided that if doing 'something different' was the new game, he would play it. He would change his brand of old wine, or at least serve it in a new bottle. And of course, he would roll out a media blitzkrieg about his new vision. He asked his secretary to set up meetings with a long list of PR consultants over the next couple of days to find a way out of this current impasse.

"What you and your production house need, sir, is rebranding. An image makeover to showcase new-age thinking," said Pranav G, a famous PR consultant as he began his presentation. What followed were a few slides of some irrelevant data and an AV that captured Hansa Productions' new-age modern image.

"Playing on your present name and carrying the legacy forward, of course, but in a brand-new avatar, relevant to young digital savvy millennials. We suggest you start a new production house called 'Black Swan Movies' or 'Black Swan

Pictures' under which these new-age line-up of films will be released," said Pranav G dramatically.

"These new films should be international, super edgy and aspirational," chirped a young girl dressed in a tight black dress that Somesh could best categorise as an attempt at sartorial representation of a Black Swan. A few logo options of the Black Swan glided on to the screen followed by some more slides on the youth, their aspirations and some edgy slogans on how Black Swan Movies would fulfil their impossible dreams.

Somesh sighed. He wanted to do something new but his hard-core film-industry training told him that the presentation made by these bright-eyed suits was no good. He was hoping to find some solutions, but it was clear that these buggers armed with iPads and Fitbits were clueless about what really worked. *Like hell I'm going to pay you crores for a change of logo and an ad campaign. I would rather make a small budget film with that money. Or launch a TV division under my banner. Maybe even an ad-film unit or something.*

Nodding in a noncommittal fashion in order to not appear like a fuddy-duddy in front of the funky, youthful team, Somesh diverted attention by serving them some fancy coffee.

"Thank you, Pranav. Superb presentation. Let me call you back," he said concluding the meeting.

*

"I need someone with that combination of new sensibility plus an understanding of what actually works in this industry. Not some hip youngsters in suits who can't look beyond their

PowerPoints. They're so in love with their own projections and their own voices that they can barely spot the problem," Somesh confided in a senior old-time producer Bittu Ranglani over a drink at the Gymkhana Club that evening.

Ranglani was sympathetic. He was a dyed-in-the-wool operator and so he said, "Somesh-bhai you need Gupta-ji."

Legend had it that Gupta-ji was a master salesman, imagemaker and strategist all rolled into one. He could, as they said, sell snow to an Eskimo. In his glory days, Gupta-ji was known to make or break careers with his conniving ways. He often had A-listers consult him on their career moves. It was not unusual to see big fancy cars parked outside his modest home in Andheri. He went by the moniker Cinema Chanakya, courtesy his unerring instinct for setting up good projects.

From devising strategies for promotion and publicity of a film, to creating stars and occasionally helping the flailing ones, Gupta-ji may well have been a professor of Hindi filmdom at a prestigious management school. But he was cut from a different cloth. Not for him the drudgery of an office job. He preferred instead the vagaries of filmdom. Its heady crests and dangerous troughs. Gupta-ji could not imagine a life without the movies and things had gone swimmingly well for a few decades for him. In fact, the seventy-something had been a go-to person for all top producers during the 1970s to the mid-1990s for advice and guidance on making their projects attractive.

Bittu Ranglani's father and after his death, Bittu Ranglani, had worked with Gupta-ji practically on all their projects. Up until five years ago when nudged by his advancing age, lack of suitable heirs, and the winds of change ushered by the arrival of the 'Studio Suits', Ranglani had been forced to shut down his film business. Gupta-ji's instincts were still as good, but he lacked the polish required to do business with the 'Suits'. And so, cutting short his once thriving career, he had retired to a neglected life in the far-flung Mumbai suburbs.

Ranglani went on to recount war stories about how Gupta-ji had worked in the trenches with him during his own production house's glory years. "Yaar Somesh-bhai, only Gupta-ji with his canny instinct can steer you through this phase. He knows the pulse of the people," Ranglani insisted.

Somesh was still hesitant. He needed someone with new thoughts, not an old fogey. "Bittu-bhai, I want fresh blood, I don't need purana chawal," said Somesh.

Ranglani smiled at Somesh's reluctance and said, "Sometimes purana chawal can become the flavour of the season."

Although reluctant, Somesh was beginning to see Bittu Ranglani's logic. Given his precarious situation, he asked tentatively, "But where is Gupta-ji these days?"

A few phone calls later, Gupta-ji was traced to a small tenement in Mira Road. When Somesh invited him to his office to discuss reviving the fortunes of his production house, Gupta-ji was noncommittal. He eventually agreed to meet Somesh as long as a car was sent to fetch him from his home in Mira Road and to drop him back.

*

"Please get Gupta-ji's favourite, a raspberry soda," Somesh instructed his peon in an attempt to make Gupta-ji feel at home as they settled down on the plush sofas in the conference room of Hansa Productions.

"Let's talk business, shall we?" said Gupta-ji, cutting to the chase.

"Yes, yes, of course, Gupta-ji. I can see that you are a no-nonsense type of person, so I'll get straight to the point. As you are aware, many new production houses have come up and our banner hasn't delivered hits for a while. And now, I'm having a lot of trouble in setting up my next film. None of the so-called 'happening' young stars want to touch my projects with a barge pole."

"May I speak to you frankly?" Gupta-ji asked, but even before Somesh could answer, he continued in his brusque manner. "To be honest, you and your production house are in the pits as of now. Right?"

Ranglani had told Somesh that Gupta-ji barely ever minced his words. But, even that warning was not sufficient to soften the blow of Gupta-ji's harsh words. Yet Somesh decided to continue to humour him.

"Gupta-ji, you know how big our banner is. We have made so many hit films..."

"All those days of glory are well behind us, today Hansa Productions is on the bottom rung," said Gupta-ji in his matter-of-fact manner.

Somesh was taken aback but he smiled through gritted teeth. "What would you suggest, *toh hum ab aage kya karein*?"

"Well, if you are at the bottom rung, you must think like a film-maker from the bottom rung. They have a simple formula. Get unknown names from small towns to star in the film, and then dress it up with some sex and sleaze and maad-dhaad. And before the release of the film, generate some controversy around it. Then look for ways to make the controversy socially relevant. *Iss* se *picture garam ho jaati hai*. Why don't you do something like this?"

Somesh looked at him wondering if this meeting was a bad idea. Then, in the most patient-sounding tone that he could manage, he said, "Gupta-ji, you know that my banner Hansa Productions does not make films with sex and violence."

"So, you still want to make only love stories?"

"Yes."

"And why is that such a problem, take newcomers and announce the film. This is an evergreen formula used by veteran established producers since time immemorial."

"Erm … because studios don't want to fund a film with newcomers. They want stars," countered Somesh.

Without missing a beat, Gupta-ji put things in perspective, "But you are facing a problem getting stars for your films. Then, why do you want to make only love stories?"

"*Kyunki pyar … yaane ki* love is an eternal emotion. Young or old, everyone understands the feeling of love. And that is what Hansa Productions is famous for. Love has always been our winning formula," said Somesh emphatically.

Gupta-ji nodded in understanding, "That reminds me of the song … *lyrics kya tha … haan … 'Shaam savere dil me mere love ka keeda hai'* …"

Somesh didn't say anything. *The man is senile. Just my luck*, he thought to himself.

Then with a dramatic flourish of his hand Gupta-ji said, "Then we have to be smart about this. We have to use the best elements of all tried-and-tested formulas and make our own special formula. And our formula will be called *Pyar mein keeda. Pyar …yaane ki love. Keeda yaane ki* … controversy."

"*Pyar mein* controversy … what on earth!" Somesh muttered under his breath.

Gupta-ji had a beatific smile on his face as though enjoying Somesh's confusion. "Somesh-ji, you know … *woh kya kehte yeh suit-tie waale* … I think 'out-of-the-box'. I did my homework before coming here. And I would like to inform you that I have the perfect casting for your next film."

Before Somesh could respond, Gupta-ji pulled out his new smartphone and pointed to the screen. Somesh saw a glamorous photo of a striking young girl on the screen. Her picture was spliced together with a pic of the popular film star Samir Manchanda.

"Who's this?" Somesh wondered aloud.

"This is Dipali Chandra, the heroine of your next film. And she is featured here with the hero of your next film."

Somesh quickly read the headline of the news article below the photo. It declared that Dipali was a background dancer and she had had an affair with superstar Samir Manchanda. The star of course denied even being aware of her existence.

"But Gupta-ji, she's a background dancer, did you not read the article?"

"Who cares! The article says Dipali and Samir had a fling sometime back. That's what is important about her. And she is a dancer, popular enough to have been noticed by the media. Becoming a leading lady will catapult her to a different league. So if you approach her, she will agree to all your terms and conditions."

"But why will Samir Manchanda agree to do a film with her?" Somesh wondered aloud, getting more perplexed with each passing minute.

"Samir Manchanda has delivered three duds at the box-office. Besides, if memory serves me right, your father gave him the big break that made him a star overnight? He has often spoken about how well he was treated even though he was a newcomer, how your father and you always made him feel special and that he would be happy to work with you folks anytime you asked. All that goodwill is the wealth you must use now. Also, he would like the opportunity of getting Dipali to stop washing dirty linen in public. What better than agreeing to Dipali being cast opposite him?"

"But Samir has done so many love stories. He is a mature actor. He won't be a suitable choice for this project."

"Hmm … if it's a love story that you want, why not one between a mature man and a young girl. Millennials think this is quite modern. And you have a real story between them too."

Somesh hesitated. "But…"

"No ifs and buts. You must grab the opportunity."

"But won't Samir be expensive…"

"As I said, he has delivered three flops. He will jump at a good price being offered to him. What's your casting budget for the film – in case you wanted A-listers?"

"Around thirty crores," Somesh replied cautiously.

"Give all of it to Samir."

"Arrey … what about other actors … and the heroine…"

"Cast fresh actors ... Drama school aur Theatre *waale.* No remuneration needed for them ... *aap unko accha break de rahe ho na...* And Dipali ... we will pay her a token amount and put her under contract for all screen work. She has flawless skin, perfect figure so you work your marketing and *adwala* contacts and get her signed up for ads. Skin creams, fitness-related brands, etc. It will help with emoting before camera, and it will get her paid from other ad agency people's pockets. And this will also create a buzz about her before the movie is launched. Win-win strategy, *hai na*?"

"All that's okay, but what story do we have for a mismatched pair like this?"

"Arrey, you have that old hit film *Ishq Aur Pyar*. Remake that with a modern twist for the new generation. *Ishq, Pyar aur Modern Love*."

"And director?"

"Save on that cost – direct it yourself. You have produced so many films. You should be able to direct in your sleep."

"Hmm..."

"Arrey, Somesh-bhai. Don't think so much. This is a casting coup. It will generate much interest. And a remake of a hit film allows you to remix and use the popular songs ... you will have media and fan curiosity about the film even before you start shooting. Of course we will not make any grand announcements ... just let the word slip out as speculative whispers. *Aur ho gayi aapki picture garam.*"

Somesh nodded.

"And one more thing. I will get a 10 per cent bonus if the film is a hit."

Somesh smiled at Gupta-ji. The *wily old man had thought through all the angles even before coming for the meeting. And his plan just might work*, he thought.

"Okay, Gupta-ji. Let's do it."

*

Dipali couldn't believe her ears when she heard from Somesh Hanswani's secretary, inviting her for a meeting at Hansa Productions' swank Juhu office to meet Somesh Hanswani and his chief PR advisor Gupta-ji.

Dressed casually in torn jeans and a blingy T-shirt knotted at the waist, Dipali made heads turn as she stepped into the office.

Somesh observed this from the one-way glass of his cabin as he watched the peon usher her to the conference room.

Gupta-ji and Somesh entered the conference room shortly. Gupta-ji spoke in the most benign manner. "Hello, Dipali-ji. I am Rakesh Gupta and this is the well-known producer now donning director's hat as well, Mr Somesh Hanswani. We are very impressed with your work. You have, what we call the X factor, and so we thought of calling you for a screen test for our next film."

"Sir! This is such an honour that you wanted to meet me. I can't believe it," Dipali said breathlessly, bending down to touch their feet, a trick she had learnt observing actresses around their heroes and directors on the set.

"Oh no … no. Please take a seat," said Somesh.

Gupta-ji suddenly took out his mobile phone and clicked on the camera on video mode.

"Ek minute ... Dipali ... Could you just show us how you would react to a phone call informing you that you have just landed a part in Somesh Hanswani's film opposite, say, Samir Manchanda?"

"Oh yes, certainly," Dipali said. She closed her eyes for a second and then enacted her surprise. An enthusiastic whoop of joy, then did a quick full cartwheel followed by some goofy dance steps to highlight her happiness and of course, that she was a brilliant and agile dancer in step with the present times.

Gupta-ji smiled.

"Somesh-bhai, this screentest video will be viral by this evening."

If Somesh was impressed at Gupta-ji's grasp of modern publicity hacks, he didn't show it. "A little over the top but we can work with her I think. Gupta-ji, you were right," said Somesh.

Dipali was happy too. She could guess that they had liked her. The Hansa Productions banner may have lost some of its sheen but it was still a big name and a modern remake of *Ishq Aur Pyar* regardless of its box-office performance would give her respectability even though she would get paid peanuts for the film. What was particularly exciting for her was that they were keen to manage her as a talent and get her signed up for ads even before the film. That was a massive bonus. They had thought this through and seemed invested in her and that was good news if Samir didn't block her.

After Dipali left, Somesh and Gupta-ji discussed the strategy to rope in Samir.

Gupta-ji said, "I've already broached the subject at the Kumars' party last night. Samir Manchanda is a decent man.

He's ready to do a film with you. You need to meet him personally to talk about it but he will agree. As long as we are generously giving him thirty crores upfront."

"And what about his past with Dipali?"

"Yes, that is still a bit of an issue. He has agreed to most things but he seems keen to bring another girl as the heroine. A family friend's daughter, I think. But don't worry, it will work out. We will convince him one way or the other," Gupta-ji reassured Somesh.

A couple of days later, Gupta-ji brought in makeover specialist Rob Ribeiro and fashion photographer Varun Burman. They did a photo session with Dipali. The results were promising. Without losing precious time, Gupta-ji released the pictures in the media with the headline HANSA PRODUCTIONS' NEW FIND: DIPALI THE DUCKLING WHO'S NOW A SWAN!

A couple of days later, Gupta-ji gave the good news to Somesh.

"Samir has agreed to do the film with Dipali. The public reaction to the article and her new makeover pics made him change his mind and see her potential in a project like this. I promised him that we will groom her further and the constant interactions with the advertising crowd will only help make her shine. Fortunately, this affair with Dipali was a casual fling so there's no really serious baggage there. He's ready to wipe the slate clean."

And so began the making of Somesh's next film production and his directorial debut. Shooting the film did not prove difficult. As things progressed, Somesh was finally feeling happy again. The project was shaping up well and within the budget. He could see redemption around the corner. Gupta-ji had delivered on his promise of putting together a good star cast.

But, as soon as the production began drawing to a close, Somesh started to worry about sending his film out in the world. In a social-media-driven world, with hardnosed entrenched publicists, would Gupta-ji's publicity strategies work? As was the case with many love story films, rumours of the lead pair in a romantic relationship had worked wonders. And it was precisely the strategy Somesh was himself thinking of. After all, it had been a success with the original lead pair of *Ishq Aur Pyar* so many years back.

Gupta-ji had, however, abandoned his earlier plan of using Samir and Dipali's romantic liaison. "Somesh-bhai, you have to understand that Samir's fling with Dipali has already been milked before the film began. It was great to spark curiosity at the start but it will not work again."

Though Somesh was convinced about his 'lead-pair-in-love' strategy, he didn't want to cross Gupta-ji openly. So he began to shut him out of important decisions and discussions. He went as far as to actively avoid meeting Gupta-ji and communicating with him via text messages and through his PA.

Somesh was stressed as he needed this film to land perfectly, he needed to get the studios on board to acquire the film to ensure a worldwide distribution. It would mean that his financial books continued to be in the pink of their health. The famous Greenlight Studios that he had been desperately wooing were in the middle of considering another film, that too a love story. Somesh wanted to show his film to the people at Greenlight, but he knew that in the pre-release phase, it would just be the publicity that could swing it for him. Showing the studio too much of the film was risky. What if they didn't like it? They would just walk away. Somesh couldn't afford that.

Pacing around in the office, he noticed that Dipali had dropped by. She had been summoned for a special photoshoot for a brand of face cream that had snapped her up as the brand ambassador. At least this part of Gupta-ji's strategy was paying dividends. They were getting a percentage of Dipali's earnings from various assignments.

"Sir, could I see you for a minute?" It was Dipali standing at Somesh's cabin door.

"Yes, sure, Dipali."

"Sir, please don't think I am being too big for my boots but I just saw your publicity strategy. Please don't mind me saying this, but it sounds terribly old-fashioned. Hinting at a romance between actors before a film's release is so passé and done to death. And besides we already played up the affair angle before the film began."

"Erm ... okay, what would you suggest?" Somesh could barely keep the irritation out of his voice.

"Sir ... I have something in mind. You are a modern progressive man so I think you will take it in the right spirit..."

"Go on." Somesh braced himself. He was almost at the end of his tether. Even small things had become too stressful for him. Greenhorn millennials with no idea of the business now had ideas to promote a film. What had the industry come to?

"Sir, I thought, why not go against the rules and try an edgy way to do this? The cheeky millennial way? After all they are your audience. In this day of streaming, people don't want *ghisa-pita* promotions."

Somesh listened intently as Dipali began to roll out what she believed would work. He knew he couldn't say anything that would create any negativity at this juncture. So he parried with the reply he knew would stop Dipali's silliness in its tracks.

"Okay. Let me think about it and speak with Samir too. You know as the hero he has to be on board for this to work."

"I've already done that, sir. But please you too should definitely speak with him," replied Dipali with a smile.

That night he couldn't sleep at all. He kept tossing and turning, running through Dipali's idea again and again in his head. The next morning, Somesh was both excited and fearful. This was the day of the big press conference that would make or break this movie. He called Dipali and Samir and asked them to just stick to his plan. He was careful, of course, not to upset either of them before the big day, even praising Dipali's initiative and Samir's cooperation. But for this round, they were better off going the traditional route. Gupta-ji too was instructed to check on all details and prep the stars well for the event. Somesh did not want to leave anything to chance.

When Somesh arrived at the multiplex which was the designated venue for the press conference of their film, he found it buzzing. Gupta-ji had done well with ensuring the numbers when it came to media attendance. OB vans crowded the parking area and youngsters with cameras and phones on selfie-sticks were all thronging the large lobby where the press conference was set up.

The cast and team filed on to the stage and took their seats across a long table with their name cards written in front on their seats. Somesh saw a small envelope placed next to his card. *Read This Please*, someone had scrawled a note on it.

Somesh tore open the envelope and read what was written. It was from Samir saying he would stick to the plan, but would speak frankly if questioned on his link-up with Dipali. Somesh's heart skipped a beat. But he kept smiling as the perfunctory announcements were made. The press conference began innocently enough and then it happened. A young scribe popped the inevitable question.

"Dipali, you are new, but there was talk of an off-screen romance between Samir and you … is it true?

Dipali hesitated for a second and then took the mike in her hand, confidently, and said, "Yes, I am new to this industry. But believe me, I refuse to play according to the old rules. The truth is that while we did know each other at one time, shooting this film with Samir was insane and totally unromantic. On sets, he was most in love with himself. And when you watch the film carefully, there are a few scenes where he's saying 'I love you' supposedly to me, but actually off-camera there was a mirror and he was saying it to himself. And that sort of self-love, my friends, is not very attractive in a man."

Samir, not to be outdone, piped up and said, "Oh yeah, and Dipali would be my first female co-star who drank like a sailor and did not shy away from letting out a loud burp even in company. And oh yes, she snored louder than a horse during the readings because she partied through the night, all the time."

Somesh was aghast at what he had just heard Samir say, but before he could even react, Dipali snatched the mike from Samir's hands and said, "And Samir is so unchivalrous and so delicate that I would end up opening the doors for him and the ladies on the set, instead of the other way around."

Somesh wished that the earth would open under him and he could sink into the gaping hole. But there was a peal of awkward laughter among the media in attendance. What was this? Even better than the romance story, thought the gathering collectively. A fight between the lead actors – this was pure gold. The young scribes were typing away on their phones furiously.

One young blogger directed a question at Somesh. "Sir, what is your stand on all that happened?"

Somesh, who was still reeling from the washing of dirty linen between his lead pair, didn't know how to react. Luckily, being the smart operator that he was, with all the composure he could gather, he wrapped up the proceedings with a short statement, "We had two warring actors in a modern love story. So now watch the film to find out more. And if you enjoy it, we will know that we have done our jobs well. Thank you."

Somesh fumed in his conference room through the rest of the day. He wanted to give Dipali and Samir a piece of his mind for letting things get out of hand despite his instructions, but controlled himself as he knew that nothing could undo what had already been done. He read and reread the note inside the envelope on which were written the lines he had been instructed to say in his last statement at the press conference. Somesh couldn't help marvelling at their audacity. His lead pair had decided to stage manage the entire press conference pretending they had nothing to do with it! Thank god, he had retained his presence of mind. But, where was Gupta-ji? He should have known what was coming. He should have come to Somesh's rescue.

He called Gupta-ji again and again on his mobile, hoping that he could give him a tongue lashing in lieu of the stars. But this time around, Gupta-ji avoided all his calls. In frustration, Somesh switched off his mobile phone and turned up the meditative chants in an effort to calm himself.

Towards the evening, when Somesh's dark mood had somewhat subsided, he finally switched on his mobile phone. And just as he did so, it rang.

After the call ended, Somesh immediately called his assistant and asked for Gupta-ji, Dipali and Samir to be summoned for an urgent meeting.

There was silence in the cabin for a few seconds after Gupta-ji walked in with Dipali and Samir later that evening. Somesh looked at them intently for a couple of minutes. Then he broke into a sheepish smile, saying, "Wow, your strategy worked! Guess who called? Sheela Das from Greenlight Studios. To congratulate us for our 'edgy, clutter-breaking' promotion strategy. And to quote her, 'It's created a great buzz and has absolutely instant-virality. Can we meet tomorrow at your office and take things forward?'"

Before Somesh could say anything further, Samir quickly said, "Somesh-ji, they have to work out a deal with you now. Or else someone else will. Our film, and the press conference was trending on Twitter all day."

Somesh beamed and said, "Dipali, I really have to thank you for this wonderful idea."

To Somesh's surprise, Dipali said, "Sir, it was actually Gupta-ji's strategy. He knew that you were hell-bent on using your old formula and were shutting him out, so he asked me to say that it was my idea."

Samir too smiled and nodded. "And I backed them up and tipped my journalist friends to ask the right questions."

Somesh looked embarrassed. He turned to Gupta-ji who was quietly standing in the corner. Somesh was about to say something when Gupta-ji raised his hand and stopped him. He smiled benignly and said, "Somesh-bhai, congratulations. *Apni picture garam ho gayi*!"

R.I.P.

Superstar Kamal Malhotra was dead. The film industry was reeling in shock at his sudden demise.

Vishal sat at his table and thought about the first time he'd met Kamal Malhotra. He had just embarked on his career and one warm summer afternoon had found himself outside a large British-style bungalow in Bandra. He remembered quite clearly how he had glanced at his visiting card. The words embossed on the thin non-tearable plastic read 'Vishal Purohit- Senior Correspondent, *Showbiz Times*'. These were the magic words to the biggest and most barricaded gates in Bollywood.

"*Khul Ja Sim-Sim*," he had muttered under his breath as he handed the visiting card to the beefy security guard who surveyed him suspiciously.

"I am here to meet Kamal-ji and Ms Tara Chaudhury for an interview."

Vishal was at this grand house to interview Kamal and Tara Chaudhary who were promoting their first film together. Tara Chaudhary was the young upcoming star, dubbed 'Sari Siren', the dream of many a young Indian male. Kamal

Malhotra was the ever-popular superstar known for his impressive list of hit films. After his illustrious predecessor Jubilee Kumar, famous for romance, it was Kamal Malhotra who had impressed the audience with his unique brand of action-comedies.

The security guard looked at the card for a couple of seconds then picked up the intercom and dialled a number.

"*Aaj sahab busy hain*," said the security guard, putting down the phone.

Vishal raised his voice a decibel. "I have an appointment."

The security guard was unimpressed. "*Roz mujhe koi yeh line bolta hai*."

Before he could reply, he noticed Kamal Malhotra's manager Resham rushing out from the bungalow towards them.

Vishal had thrown a hissy fit. "Resham yaar, what is this? You gave my editor the appointment and your security guy has not even been told that I will be dropping in. How insulting! After all I'm from the…"

"The leading media group. Of course. I'm so sorry for the mix-up! This guard is new here. Otherwise, who doesn't know you guys at *Showbiz Times*? We are so excited that this first-page interview is finally happening."

Vishal had looked condescendingly at the security guard and said, "My photographer will be here too. Let him in."

The guard had just looked down sheepishly and nodded.

"You've gone through the film's promotional plan, right?" Resham asked eagerly.

"Of course. I do my research," Vishal lied through his teeth. He was trying very hard to stifle a yawn. He had been too busy hanging out with friends till an ungodly hour the previous night. His boss had informed him just that morning that he was to do the story. He knew Vishal hated these soft puff-piece stories and had purposely assigned him this crappy job. Vishal was more interested in stories behind the story. And he was determined to get one that day.

Resham had led Vishal up the gravelly driveway to the house. He couldn't help but marvel at the old colonial mansion with its elegant charm. The house, a prized piece of real estate, was the envy of all of Bollywood. The general film-industry version was that Kamal Malhotra had bought the house for his lady love Tara Chaudhury. The fifty-plus Malhotra, like most stars of his vintage, was married, and even had a daughter, who would be about the same age as Tara. But what's love and romance got to do with age or being married? A few months earlier, Malhotra had become besotted by the svelte Tara who was almost twenty years younger. Malhotra was believed to have said to friends that Tara was the love of his life. And then, all of a sudden he had bought this grand house as a gesture of his undying love. He'd moved out of his sprawling Juhu bungalow. There were whispers of them being secretly married, but nobody knew for sure.

Their roaring affair started, as it often does, on the sets of this very film Vishal was interviewing them for. But, nobody had really spoken openly about them as an item out of respect for Malhotra and perhaps for his wife of many years, Dolly. Everyone displayed what is known in film industry parlance as '*aankhon ki sharam*'. Whenever they saw Kamal and Tara together away from a film set, filmwalas would pretend as though the affair had never happened.

So predictably when Vishal's interview appeared it rocked the industry. The interview had been organised for promoting the film. But much to the shock of the publicist, Vishal's headline read EXPOSED: KAMAL MALHOTRA AND TARA CHAUDHURY'S LOVE NEST.

The interview was a complete departure from what Vishal had promised Kamal's PR team, with romantic details of their personal lives and a selection of candid photographs which were even more revealing. It was apparent that the strapping and handsome Kamal Malhotra, gazing into the hazel eyes of statuesque Tara Chaudhury, was in love. The interview had gone viral immediately and made it to print and online editions in different languages. And like all sensational stories, it had opened the floodgates. Vishal's story had spawned a zillion others. And after that, multiple stories about the rivalry between Dolly Malhotra and Tara Chaudhury had been scooped, planted and made viral.

That had been a few years ago. After which, Kamal rode the wave of public interest masterfully, and his stardom actually scaled greater heights. Instead of being vilified, Tara's popularity too had soared. The couple became the darlings of the masses. Those were good times. But alas, good times don't last. Kamal Malhotra, who had been making back-to-back films with Tara, suddenly signed a film with another upcoming starlet. Obviously it got everyone wondering. Was Kamal and Tara's affair over? Rumours of Tara's liaison with a younger male co-star had also been doing the rounds.

But, the latter appeared to be the standard movie marketing trick and Vishal had not thought much of it. In fact, he dismissed that as just a silly rumour and believed Tara when she crossed her heart and swore to him that nothing untoward had happened between her and Kamal. "Vishal, sweetheart, you will be the first to know if anything happens in my life. You have a special place in my heart, you know that," she had trilled in one of their phone interviews.

Vishal had believed her; a fatal mistake for a film journalist. And as night follows the day, he missed a big scoop. His rival, Mufeed, from the city's leading tabloid, beat him to it, revealing to the world that good sense had prevailed and Kamal Malhotra had moved back to his home to be with wife Dolly and daughter Avani.

Nobody cared enough to look beyond the sensational headline, but Vishal had been keeping a watch on developments even though Malhotra had refused his requests for interviews and Tara continued to pretend as though nothing in their equation had changed. According to Tara, Kamal just wanted to spend a little time with his daughter. Never in her life would Tara admit that Kamal had left her and gone back to Dolly. That would be admitting that Dolly had won.

Dolly, quite understandably, reciprocated Tara's dislike for her. To her, Tara was the epitome of a backstabber. In fact, it was Dolly who had introduced Tara to her husband at a party. Tara Chaudhury had been a young newbie who had somehow wormed her way into a kitty party group that Dolly belonged to. Tara had befriended Dolly and even called her Didi. In fact they became thick as thieves, and given their sisterly equation Dolly thought it safe to introduce her to the husband. Dolly had recommended Tara for a couple of films that Kamal was producing but not acting in. Tara was flighty, but Dolly expected that she would show loyalty and gratitude for pushing her into the big league. The first few movies went by uneventfully, but then Kamal cast her opposite himself. It was during an outdoor in Paris that all hell broke loose. Dolly was informed by Kamal's man Friday Shankar to come to Paris immediately. "It is urgent madam," was all Shankar had said.

When Dolly had reached the hotel in Paris, unannounced, she was shocked to find Tara's suite adjacent to Kamal's, complete with a common door. She knew exactly what that meant. Dolly was shattered not so much by her husband's dalliance. He was a man and a star at that. She expected him to cheat but she was incensed at Tara's betrayal. She was supposed to be in Dolly's camp and protect her interest. And soon after, adding insult to injury, Kamal had bought Tara a house and moved out of their family home. It was a humiliation that had diminished Dolly's status as the star wife. Even industry underlings had started treating her with pity and scorn. Ever since, the two women had been on a warpath. Dolly had barely managed to somehow pull herself together only after Mrs Kumar, Bollywood's Queen Bee and surviving matriarch of a large film family, called her home.

After an exchange of polite pleasantries in the manicured lawns of her well-appointed home, Mrs Kumar came straight to the point. "Don't worry. He will come back. They always do. Meanwhile, look after yourself to be ready to welcome him when he does. I will give you the number for my beautician – she has the magic touch. Meet with her and she will do the needful."

Mrs Kumar had been right. Kamal had returned home. Although the reasons for the reconciliation had been kept secret by Dolly.

And now suddenly out of the blue, news of Kamal Malhotra's death in New York had broken out. The events leading up to his demise had followed the script of filmi lives. Kamal had collapsed while filming in New York. He was rushed to the hospital, but passed away soon after. Apparently, he had suffered a massive heart attack.

As it turned out, the reality was quite different. Kamal had spent almost all his fortune on Tara by giving her a fancy house and a luxurious lifestyle. He then returned home in poor health, much less capable of playing the lead in too many films, because he had been suffering from cancer. The advancing years had set in and the cancer was making him degenerate faster. However, Dolly, who had taken him back, refused to be taken for a ride this time. She made it clear that she would look after all his creature comforts, his health, everything, but the responsibility of their family's financial well-being rested on his shoulders.

Kamal got the hint. Realising the gravity of the situation he had decided it was best for once to unquestioningly go with the wife's wishes. And so he continued to work, to keep their family home up and running – with the cars, the liveried staff and an affluent lifestyle – till he just could not. The pain had become excruciating. He knew he needed the best of medical help and America seemed like the best option for privacy. So he had set up a long outdoor shoot in New York. With the hope of covering up his treatment. But, obviously he could not. Things had gone from bad to worse to tragic.

*

Before anyone could react to the news of Kamal's death, Dolly, in keeping with Kamal's last wishes, along with their daughter and a few relatives, conducted Kamal's funeral and cremated him in the US itself. Kamal believed that a star should always be viewed by his fans as one, and had given strict instructions to his family that no photos of his dead body should be clicked, let alone circulated. The funeral, he had insisted, should take place away from the public eye. He wanted people to remember him only as the glorious star that he was. And so, no press or media had been allowed. As per Kamal's wishes, Dolly had flown directly to Varanasi and scattered his ashes in the Ganga before heading to Mumbai.

Back home in Mumbai, Dolly was finally overcome with emotion. But grief soon turned to rage. She believed that it was typical of her husband to put his own wishes before hers right up to his last breath ... robbing her of that last moment of glory where she could remind the world of her rightful place next to him.

After she had learnt of her husband's dalliance with Tara, Dolly had taken solace in playing her role as a suffering and rightful wife with finesse. Every occasion that offered the opportunity of emphasising to the world her wifely status was Dolly's window to happiness. And respect. She had long dreamt of this moment. That should Kamal ever pass away before her – the likelihood of that being quite high, given his excessive lifestyle – she would make it a proud moment, truly reclaiming him as her own. But, her husband, as was his habit, had shattered that dream by his foolish instructions. Dolly knew that to disobey a dead man's last wishes would be sacrilege. And so the funeral had been low-key and functional with only a few family members and exactly three close friends in attendance in the US.

There must be a way out of this, Dolly thought to herself as she sat in the puja room. And in that moment, as she sent up her most sincere prayers to the heavens, she knew what to do! Organise a prayer service! It was the best way to bid her Kamal a fitting and fond farewell. A prayer service which would celebrate Kamal's life and work as a star; Kamal at his glorious best. Given Kamal's popularity, it would be a surety that the A-list of the industry would be in attendance. Smiling gratefully at the statue of Lord Ganesha before her, Dolly Malhotra started putting together the plans of the grand prayer service. Nobody was going to stop her now.

*

Initially, Vishal presumed that the prayer service was a sentimental corollary to the star's unexpected death, a last goodbye of sorts. But, then he had found a source who told him something that was contrary to what was being spoken of as the cause of Kamal's death. Vishal had been informed that Kamal Malhotra had cancer. And apparently that was the reason he'd moved back to be with Dolly. Vishal realised he needed to get the complete picture, the missing links which nobody had bothered with.

What was the cancer he was suffering from? Vishal scratched his head, trying to research on the Internet. Whatever it was, it was obviously a deadly one. Kamal had passed away within a couple of months. It was unfortunate considering his films had been doing well, his popularity soaring unlike actors his age or even younger.

Now as he entered Kamal Malhotra's family bungalow that sat at the end of a picturesque semi-private narrow lane in Juhu, Vishal wondered if he should snoop around a bit. He had deliberately reached almost forty-five minutes early in the hope of catching a break. Vishal did need a scoop. Desperately. The strange thing about most people was that while they couldn't care less when a person, especially a celebrity, was alive, news of a celebrity death would draw them to stories like sharks to blood. Anything and everything on big-ticket celebs following their deaths was sure-fire success.

*

A massive white shamiana had been erected on the sprawling lawns of the bungalow. Holy chants were resonating in the background. Vishal lingered at the entrance of the shamiana which was milling with staff in uniform and family members. Vishal hung around, looking for the right moment to question staff and sundry star chamchas.

If not for everyone attired in white and a subdued atmosphere, Vishal would have imagined this to be a high-tea sort of affair. Everywhere he looked, he could spot many decorative clusters of fragrant mogras and rajnigandhas sprinkled with just the right number of rose petals to lend a little drama to the sobriety of the occasion.

At the right corner of the shamiana the caterers were readying their fare. Classical sarod and sitar music had just begun adding to the soulful atmosphere. The white slips on the chairs, each with an ivory ribbon band, went in tandem with the overall colour theme. On the sides of the shamiana were large photo-displays of the star in his many moods, laughing, thoughtful, horsing around with one of his directors, playing cricket with the light boys, shaking hands with the former Prime Minister Manmohan Singh and one with Hillary Clinton.

At the very end of the shamiana, below a massive portrait of Kamal Malhotra which was decked with the ubiquitous white flowers, was Dolly Malhotra. *What's with film folks and white floral arrangements that look all the same*, wondered Vishal. He then turned his attention to Dolly Malhotra's ensemble. She was immaculately turned out for the service as a superstar's wife should be. Attired in a chic white linen salwar-kurta, her hair coloured an elegant shade of caramel, she made for a striking bereaved widow. All around her were the paparazzi with flashbulbs going crazy. *Ahhh! Cameras. The Pied Pipers even to celebrities in mourning*, thought Vishal.

To his surprise, through the small knot of paparazzi, Dolly's hard-as-steel gaze locked with his. Vishal was a little nonplussed but he recovered quickly. He slowly walked towards Dolly Malhotra with folded hands to convey his condolences. As he neared, she kept her eyes locked with his and said, "When do you want to do the interview?"

"Err, what?" Vishal was surprised. He hardly expected to get an exclusive with Dolly Malhotra so soon. But, lady luck seemed to be smiling on him. He could be the first to file an exclusive with Dolly. Given the heavy sentimentality surrounding Kamal Malhotra's death, chances were that Dolly's interview would go viral. And Vishal figured that Dolly knew that too. He was momentarily embarrassed about his mercenary analysis of the situation, but then the rationalist in him took over. An exclusive is an exclusive after all.

"Any time you're ready for it, Dolly-ji," he said.

Dolly Malhotra surprised Vishal again. She signalled Shankar to get Vishal seated in a private garden area adjoining the large shamiana.

Vishal couldn't believe his luck. This was fantastic. He sat on a garden chair and chatted up Shankar. "*Sir toh bilkul achanak chale gaye*..." Vishal said, trying to sound sympathetic.

Shankar nodded. He was too shrewd to say anything to a journalist.

Within a few minutes, Dolly walked in quietly and Shankar magically disappeared. Before Vishal could even ask his first question, Dolly began talking as if on autopilot. The first part of her outpouring was their magical love story and their picture-perfect marriage.

After listening to her patiently for a few minutes, Vishal ventured, "Why was Kamal-ji working in his condition?"

"Condition? What condition. Ah! You're talking about the rumours of cancer? Dear boy, how long have you been in the industry? Don't you know these kind of rumours float around after every big star's sudden demise. Kamal was fit and fine. And he wanted to spend more time with me. But, the industry could not have enough of him. They could have made those films with someone else but they only wanted him. And it's really hard to say no to friends. They are like family after all," said Dolly, dabbing her eyes softly.

Vishal could have sworn there were no tears. He realised that Dolly was not going to say anything about Kamal's cancer. He didn't dare ask her further about it.

He was about to ask his next question when out of the corner of his eye he noticed the photographers moving away rapidly out of the shamiana. Dolly could not be bothered. She continued talking, seemingly confiding in him. "In a short while, we will have Kamal's friends and colleagues pouring in and I want to be there personally to meet each one. So let us finish the interview before they arrive," she said.

"What about rumours of your husband's second wife, although he never divorced you, did he?"

Vishal thought she would squirm or be caught off-guard by his question. But all Dolly did was smile brightly. The steely glint was back in her eyes. "At the time of my husband's death we were still very much legally married so that makes any other marriage as you would know – illegal; with no societal standing. You can check the records in the Family Court in Bandra. There was no divorce between us. We were a happily married showbiz couple. My husband was a star with a larger-than-life image that he had to live up to. But he was very innocent. He couldn't say no to a woman who shamelessly threw herself at him. But that silly mistake didn't mean anything. I knew that he would always come back to me – the mother of his child, his legally wedded wife." She said the words with relish and a smile as though it was an inside joke.

"Hmm … but what about the fact that he had moved in with Tara Chaudhury for some time? They are rumoured to have tied the knot. I believe she too had wanted to be present at the funeral but you decided to keep her out?"

"The funeral was in keeping with Kamal's wishes … strictly for family, darling," Dolly shot back unfazed. "The woman you're referring to was just a PR stunt for Kamal. She has no place here. It was just a convenient link-up for the media to lap up. It made for good headlines and helped sell his movies to the audience. He wrapped that chapter up when it died its natural death. But you already know that. Don't you?"

"Fair enough, but she was a colleague so I presume she will be here for the prayer service?" Vishal persisted.

After a dramatic pause, Dolly launched forth again, totally ignoring Vishal's question. "As I was saying, Kamal's death is an unimaginable loss for us – the family but an even bigger one for his fans and which is why, I have decided to keep his legacy alive through a memorial trust dedicated to him which will produce films and grow new film talent. I want you to write about that," she said, her voice authoritative with a gravelly husk of a habitual smoker.

Dolly looked at him with an expression that bordered on the sad and tragic, but Vishal knew it was well rehearsed, "I can count on your help, right?" she asked. "It's difficult for us and we need bright young journalists like you to help us to remind people of Hindi cinema's glorious past. I am speaking exclusively to you because I like your work."

"Of course," Vishal shot back facetiously. He knew she was bullshitting him, but nevertheless, he felt flattered. She had rarely done interviews and this could be a real scoop if she gave details of the trust and the big event lined up.

She did. In fact she did one better, and promised to share with him old photos of her and Kamal as a young couple together. "My office will email you the scanned photos but I want a cover story, ok?"

Suddenly, glancing at her watch discreetly, Dolly looked around and noticed that the shamiana was still bereft of any VIP presence.

"Where is everyone?" she blurted out to no one in particular. She appeared anxious and stopped their conversation abruptly to summon Shankar.

"Where are the expected guests? Should they not be here by now?" she said, the quiet anger making her gravelly voice menacing.

"Err ... madam about that, need to talk with you ... since you were busy with the interview..." Shankar sputtered nervously.

Vishal sat looking down at the Dictaphone while straining his ears to catch their conversation.

Shankar whispered in her ear and she sprang out of her seat like a long-suppressed Jack-in-the-Box.

She turned to Vishal, her livid face a far cry from the aggrieved mourning widow she had looked like just a few moments ago. But, when she spoke she was all milk and honey once more. "The prayer service will start soon. We will talk afterwards, darling, and finish the interview. Maybe tomorrow."

Vishal was crushed. He wanted to file today, but she hadn't given him anything that could go viral. He cursed under his breath on his way out. Then he noticed that the shamiana was really quite bare. *Where is everyone*? he thought, stepping out of the bungalow into the narrow lane that led to the main road. He saw that there was a massive crowd gathered at a short distance away at the mouth of the lane.

He walked towards the crowd surging around a beautiful young woman also dressed in a white salwar kurta standing on the pavement outside the small florist shop at the corner of the lane. It was Tara Chaudhury. She was a sight to behold with fresh yellow flowers held in her hand adding to her beauty. The crowd had thickened into an unruly mob on both sides of the road but Tara was being shielded on the pavement by a chain of hefty bouncers. A host of paparazzi were busy clicking away and Tara was obliging them by posing. A long line of Jaguars and Bentleys was stuck in the crowd. Behind them was a massive traffic jam that snaked for about half a kilometre along the main road. It was a juicy moment for fans who wanted to get a glimpse of the famous superstar's glamorous young mistress as she made her way to the prayer service hosted by his wife. And, Tara Chaudhury was giving them their *paisa-wasool* moment by standing on the road outside the superstar's house with folded hands, greeting them.

Soon the line of VIP cars was about a kilometre long, leaving some actors no option but to get out of their cars and walk towards Kamal Malhotra's bungalow. But, as soon as they did that they began to get mobbed too. After all these were Bollywood's A-list celebs. Tara Chaudhury's personal security was quick. They pulled in the VIPs onto the pavement outside the flower shop and pushed the crowds back. The VIPs who were stuck on the pavement had no option but to stand next to Tara and wait around for the crowds to disperse. Now the entire area was jammed. It would be impossible to open it for the cars to pass through the sea of humanity.

A massive photograph of Kamal Malhotra on a roll-up standee appeared from inside the boot of a car which seemed to belong to Tara Chaudhury. Chaudhury's staff put up the standee right next to where she stood on the pavement. With an exaggerated gesture she laid the flowers from the florist shop on the ground in front of the standee. A megaphone was handed to Tara Chaudhury and she loudly announced that fans could pay their respects to the star if they filed in an orderly queue before the standee. She stood next to the standee and accepted the condolences. Other members of the media pushed their way through the crowds and began to livestream the proceedings. It made for a memorable photo op, top Bollywood stars standing with Tara Chaudhury on a pavement, along with crowds, paying their respects to the dearly departed Kamal Malhotra.

Vishal, who had also made his way almost to where Tara stood, suddenly noticed the crowd parting. Dolly Malhotra strode towards Tara. *This is too good. Way beyond my expectation*, Vishal thought to himself. He was about to witness a massive catfight. But as Dolly arrived in front of the florist's shop her features were composed and she looked as graceful and demure as possible. Surely she wasn't going to let Tara Chaudhury steal her legacy, her moment, her grand prayer service. Tara had appropriated her husband, but this was Dolly's moment of assertion that Kamal belonged to her and not Tara.

When the two women came face to face, Dolly clasped Tara's folded hands and embraced her in an unexpected hug. The crowd was surprised, but cheered. The photographers and cameramen went wild with excitement. Seizing the moment, Dolly took the megaphone from Tara and thanked everyone for their support. She then looked at Tara and said, "We may have fought in the past but a prayer service for my husband even if it's held on the roads is sacred for me. Sister, let this be a fond send-off from both of us and all those who loved him." There was a deafening applause.

Then suddenly the crowd went silent. Everyone was waiting for Tara's response. Vishal could swear that for once Tara was struggling with her thoughts. Suddenly, she bent down and touched Dolly's feet, making the crowd go hysterical with excitement once again. When she arose, there were tears streaming down her face. She took the mike from Dolly's hands and started on a moving speech about Kamal Malhotra.

"Undoubtedly it is Kamal's soul that made this coming together of his loved ones possible. I am so indebted to Dolly-di for joining me on this occasion. As per his last wishes, I would like to formally announce the formation of my trust, The Kamal Cine Foundation, which aims to give back to the industry and the people that keep it running."

Vishal sucked in his breath. Didn't Dolly tell him just a few minutes back that she was planning a trust in Kamal's name? Tara had clearly upstaged Dolly again. Vishal glanced at Dolly who looked stricken. Tara, confident that she had crushed her adversary, announced grandly, adding insult to injury, "And … I would also like to invite her to head this foundation and be its chief trustee."

Tara looked triumphant, but she had underestimated Dolly, expecting her to drop the act and walk away in a huff. For a long moment Dolly remained silent as though overcome by emotions. She knew how to play the victim to the hilt. Nothing could take that away from her. Wiping her eyes, Dolly cleared her throat and spoke.

"If there is anything that Kamal-ji has taught me, it is to never decline a chance to work for the greater good. I accept Tara's offer in all humility and hope to serve the film industry. And I want to add that I will ensure that all proceeds from Kamal's cinematic works will go into this endeavour."

The crowd clapped louder and louder at Dolly's generosity, unaware that a good amount of Kamal's income from films starring him and Tara actually went to the latter!

Tara was struggling to look as composed as she had done a few minutes ago. But, before she could stabilise herself, Dolly switched off the megaphone and briskly moved towards Tara and hugged her tight. Tara too burst into a beaming smile for the benefit of the surrounding cameras. Dolly's smile was benign. It was indeed an unforgettable moment, a moment that belonged to the best cinema Bollywood could conjure.

*

Vishal Purohit had his lead story the next day. R.I.P – TARA CHAUDHURY AND DOLLY MALHOTRA'S ENMITY IS NOW DEAD. Who says women can't bury the hatchet and be friends for the greater good!

And yes, that story and the picture did go viral!

But had the megaphone mike been on the previous evening, Vishal would surely have heard Dolly whispering in Tara's ear, "You backstabber, I'm going to take back every paisa Kamal ever gave to you." And Vishal would also have heard Tara whisper back, "Good to see that you're still a bitter and miserable witch."

Sibling Saga

A loud shriek and the sound of glass crashing on the floor could be heard across the sprawling bungalow grounds in Goa. It was Aryaa Bedi, the once uber-glamorous Hindi film heroine, venting.

At the height of her career, which began at the cusp of the new millennium and extended to the mid-2010s, she was famously known as the Glam Diva. As the title suggests, Aryaa was not as well-known for her onscreen performance, as she was for her very urbane and chic style inspired by Hollywood – à la Audrey Hepburn meets Julia Roberts if you please. Her diction, with a pronounced convent-educated accent, only added to the Western aura and unintentionally created a style of dialogue delivery that was emulated by young aspirants long after Aryaa's prime. Industry watchers always felt that she was one helluva lucky brat because despite being a total misfit in the Hindi film heroine mould she had captivated her audience merely with a charming personality.

Apart from being a former style icon and superstar, Aryaa was also an heiress to a movie empire, courtesy her bright and talented father, producer K.K. Bedi, who had ever the keen eye for talent. When Aryaa was a mere teen, her father realized quickly enough that Aryaa's elfin charm impressed everyone she met. He began to groom her for a career in the movies. But Aryaa, all of seventeen back then, wasn't sure whether she wanted to be in showbusiness. She had always dreamt of going to the United States, Harvard University to be precise, to study business management. Acting, to her, was an absolute no-no. She had seen enough of the glamorous life, the wild parties, the crazy affairs, the adulation, and the eventual, inevitable fall from grace. Her parent's marriage, she thought, was the perfect example of the destructive power of showbusiness.

At the time that K.K. Bedi was trying to convince his naïve daughter to give films a shot, his own career in the business was in jeopardy. He was in financial doldrums. Given his problem with alcohol, he was on the expressway downhill and he needed a miracle to resurrect himself. In short, he needed to produce a film out of thin air, as he had no money. He was heavily in debt and at this juncture none of his friends were ready to work with him. However, given all the goodwill he had with colleagues, a few were willing to loan him some money to bail him out. But what he really needed was fresh, new talent at zero cost, some great music and the generosity of his distributors to tide over this rough patch.

Serendipitously, it was around this time when he realized that his seventeen-year-old daughter Aryaa would be the perfect candidate for his resurrection. She was good-looking and young, a breath of fresh air. Casting her would be a coup of sorts. Bedi directing his own daughter would be big enough news for the press and take care of the publicity of the film. And the best part of it would be that the bright, shiny new star would come free of any cost!

Now the tricky part was convincing Aryaa. But K.K. Bedi had a trick up his sleeve. He knew his darling daughter well. And so, he made her read the part he had in mind for her, pretending that he wanted her feedback for that elusive 'youth connect' for the movie. Aryaa had loved the script and given some honest feedback to help improve it.

In the course of their improv discussion, K.K. casually let slip, sighing dramatically for effect, "Beta Aryaa, it's a pity you don't want to act because you and I both know what a meaty role this is. Anyway, I don't want to force this on you, so I am going to offer this role to Vanita Kishan. She is a big star's daughter, very pretty and seems keen to be an actress. Of course, I will have to pay a heavy price to rope her in."

Aryaa found herself feeling shocked and disappointed at this unexpected turn of events when, actually, she should have been relieved. Perhaps, she had expected her father to wear her down with his pleading till she finally gave in to his wishes. Besides, to be honest, the role was quite appealing, one which would not make her squirm in her shoes or cringe.

Her head was a mix of guilt and embarrassment at that moment as she let her imagination run riot and conjured up a scenario wherein her departure to the US had led to K.K. Bedi's eventual ruin and bankruptcy! Being young and somewhat the sentimental type, Aryaa could not bear the guilt of not being there for her daddy in his hour of need. "Okay, Dad, I will do this one only to help you, but promise me that you will let me go to Harvard after this?" she blurted out.

Bedi, of course, had been banking on this change of heart all along. He was merely surprised that it had taken Aryaa so long to make up her mind.

Hiding his gleeful smile, looking suitably impressed and thoughtful, after a dramatic pause, he gazed lovingly at his daughter and said, "Of course, beta, I am willing to send you to Harvard or Oxford tomorrow itself. You know that."

Aryaa made an impressive debut and the movie earned just about enough for everyone to get paid, along with a healthy bonus. But it was the glowing gushing praise from critics and trade pundits which signalled that K.K. Bedi's career had just received a new lease of life. And thus a shiny new star was born in tinseltown.

As K.K. Bedi had anticipated, Aryaa's plans for Harvard were put on the backburner as she got busy with the next film, and then the next, all directed by her father. The profits had started swelling given Aryaa's popularity and before she knew it, Bedi Productions was among the top five production houses in Bollywood.

*

The next fifteen years were a blur. While on the professional front the family fortunes remained steady, on the personal front K.K. Bedi's marriage was on the rocks. After a surprisingly quick and hassle-free divorce from his first wife, also Aryaa's mother, he moved on to a new bride. By now Aryaa was thirty-two, just about to sail into the 'senior actress' category.

With her father preoccupied with work and his new family she felt it was a good time to get married. Fortuitously, that's when Aryaa herself found love. Soon she tied the knot with a bohemian musician Victor Da Cunha and moved to Goa. She decided to focus on her marriage and let her career take a back seat.

The years as a leading actress had been both exhilarating and stressful. During those years, she knew her father was banking on her to resurrect his career and consolidate it so that he could build a studio. Aryaa had done her bit. She was so consumed by her desire to prove herself as capable as him that she had not spared a thought to her own ambitions and dreams.

Her life on the island of Divar in Goa was as blissful and idyllic as it could be. Initially, Aryaa had felt that Victor, a complete free spirit, was the perfect match for her. They had been introduced at a rock show where Victor was one of the star performers and his trippy care-a-damn style swept her off her feet. They had some things in common too, like their love for music and she understood the demands of a performer's life, so they had managed to strike a harmonious balance. Or that's what Aryaa thought. Until she found out about his penchant for one-night stands and his secret, drug dependency. Bitter fights became the norm at their Divar island home. Soon Aryaa was too exhausted to fight her husband and so she just distanced herself, finding comfort in the bottle, just as her father had done.

When Aryaa's alcohol dependency became public knowledge, the very same media who once loved her turned on her and she was conveniently dubbed 'Alkie Aryaa' by the tabloids. And then, to add to her troubles, Victor, while he was away on a tour, once again sprung an unpleasant surprise on her quite like the time he had come home with a groupie. But this time it was far worse. Victor had died. As the news of his death caused by drug overdose came in, Aryaa was both shattered and secretly relieved.

After the mourning friends and family had gone and the grieving had abated, Aryaa was left wondering what she would do with her life. She spoke to her father at length and he had promised he would come up with something.

"Don't worry, beta. You are my baby, my family. There will always be room for you once you get over this," K.K. Bedi had reassured his grieving daughter, confident that Aryaa would take a while to pivot back.

After his departure, Aryaa took a long and hard look at herself in the mirror. The alcohol had taken its toll and she had put on weight. Thankfully, however, her blessed genes had stopped her from becoming excessively fat. She knew she had to act quickly, before she disappeared again from the headlines.

The upside of Victor's death was that it nudged Aryaa into taking charge of her life. There were no more excuses for completely letting herself go. She started cycling extensively, an activity she usually undertook after her fights with Victor. Goa's rolling and picturesque landscape gave her ample room to cycle away from thoughts of her dreary, failed and tragic relationship. That act of escape and rebellion had somewhat kept the ravages of alcohol in check on her contours. As for the other problems, luckily, they all fell within the ambit of issues that science could solve. She made a quick mental note to speak with her doctor.

However, during this time of introspection and self-improvement, when the alcohol-induced haze had subsided, Aryaa also began to notice that she now had competition from the most unexpected quarter – her own family!

Her younger, better-looking step-sibling, Prerna Bedi, had been making waves with her selfies on Instagram.

Scrolling through Twitter and Instagram to check out her competition, she discovered that it was her stepsister – whom Aryaa secretly called her 'NemeSis' – had now officially been declared as the face of the Bedi banner!

It was around the time of this life-altering discovery that Aryaa's neighbours on Divar heard the crashing sound of the bottles.

*

Aryaa felt betrayed. Why, K.K. Bedi had met her just a couple of months back at Victor's funeral, but he did not breathe a word of his plans with Prerna.

She raved and ranted to herself, "Why did Daddy not consult me on this? After all, wasn't the new improved version of his production house built on the back of my popularity and youth?" Even Victor's philandering had not hurt so much.

In a rage, she dialled K.K. Bedi's number on her phone.

"Dad, what the fuck is this? Prerna is the face of the banner now? Not me? How could you do this sneaking behind my back?"

"Beta, you were busy with your marriage and family these past few years. And let's face it, you yourself decided to give up acting, didn't you? Wasn't it you who said, 'Dad, I've been there and done that' – your words, not mine."

Aryaa was speechless for a minute. Damn! She did say all that. It sounded like a great sign-off line back then but now she wished she hadn't. However, being K.K. Bedi's daughter, she was never at a loss for words for too long.

"Dad, I had said those things earlier too, but you always found a way to make me change my mind or rather made me realize what I really wanted. This time you didn't. Why? Because you felt that I had outlived my utility. And with a shiny new daughter in the family, you had options, right, unlike the last time?"

He could hear Aryaa sobbing on the phone. Bedi realized that for someone struggling with alcohol issues, Aryaa was particularly sharp and astute. He knew all about her problems even though she hadn't discussed it with him. Of course, he had gone through the dark phase himself and come out of it, in no small measure because of Aryaa. Now this touching, unshakeable faith of hers that Daddy would make her topsy-turvy life right was moving, but also a little cloying. And needy. He would have to think of a way out of this one, otherwise there was no telling what Aryaa would do.

"Come to Mumbai, beta, let's fix things," he boomed, reassuring her in his gruff Papa Bear voice.

*

Four weeks later, Aryaa was in Mumbai. As she walked out of the airport, she noticed that her father was there to receive her personally. It was a good sign.

K.K. Bedi knew it was important to keep Aryaa in a good mood through this phase. Good for her, the family and yes, of course, business. The business was at a critical juncture and he could not afford a family drama. Observing from a distance, he was impressed by what he saw. Aryaa was looking good and getting plenty of second glances. Gone was the puffiness that he had seen on his visit during Victor's funeral in Goa. She was looking almost as good as when she had left, even if a tad overweight.

They hugged for the cameras lined outside the airport before getting into the white Mercedes awaiting them.

"This seems to be brand new," said Aryaa.

"Yes, it is. And it's yours," replied Bedi, expansively.

"Wow, Daddy! Thanks."

"Anything for my dearest, Aryaa Beta," he said.

Bedi patted himself in his mind for getting off to a good start, but he knew things could get rough later. It was too early to celebrate.

And sure enough, Aryaa's biting questions followed quick and fast. A bitter smile on her face, she asked him, "Is this one of your guilt gifts? What are you hiding?"

"Nothing to hide," he said cheerily and then finally decided to stop bullshitting his eldest progeny.

"Look, Bedi Productions will be announcing a big film with Prerna tomorrow – she is the heroine. This had been in the works for a while." And before Aryaa could respond, he added hastily, "But given that our favourite

Bedi, Aryaa, is back in town, we will announce a film that you will be directing!"

Aryaa shot back, "So this is Daddy Bedi informing me that there is no vacancy for me in front of the camera."

"C'mon, Aryaa Beta. It's fair to both of you. Prerna gets to do what she does best at her age and you, my eldest progeny, take on my mantle, the director's mantle. You'll be the first woman to direct for the banner, and all that blah-blah that we'll feed to the media. It will be a good comeback and given the circumstances, nobody will be unforgiving. As an actress, there will be too many comparisons, unfair ones, unkind ones with the new-generation girls."

Aryaa heard him out quietly. "Sure. I understand," she said. There was no point arguing with the old man. He always chose business over emotions, and she was, after all, his daughter. She would do the same thing.

*

As soon as she was in her old apartment, Aryaa started working the phones. The first call she made was to her ex-flame Vijay Khanna. They had both started out at the same time and were a hit pair at one time. People loved seeing them together in movies. But a silly spat between Vijay and her father had made the 'Hit Jodi' fall apart. Vijay had been kicked out of a film years ago by K.K. Bedi for demanding a larger-than-expected fee and a proper bound script. In return, Vijay had badmouthed KK in film circles. As a result, KK had nursed a deep hatred for Vijay, a fact that he could not reveal openly because of Vijay's star status.

But now, Vijay was the Numero Uno star, and had been in the top spot for close to a decade with over thirty superhits and counting. To add to this, Aryaa knew that Vijay was a master strategist when it came to playing and manipulating the film *industrywalas* to his advantage.

Despite the fallout between Vijay and KK, Aryaa had remained in touch with the former, albeit secretly. They'd had a fling in the beginning of their pairing and still had a soft spot for each other. Of course, Vijay had moved on with a string of girlfriends half his age, but their bond had remained strong. Aryaa could not think of anyone but Vijay to call for advice on her future, which at the moment looked extremely shaky. She could sense that too much had changed, and she'd have to navigate her way carefully to make a successful comeback.

They spoke for a long time, well past midnight, and Aryaa felt a lot better, but even more nervous. Vijay had given her plenty to think about with suggestions for future projects. He had also confirmed her worst fears. Through the industry grapevine, he was aware of the developments in the family business and also that her home banner was now going to be represented by her stepsister Prerna.

"Nothing succeeds like success in showbusiness, Aryaa, and you've got to admit that Prerna is becoming a favourite in the inner filmi circles. Other banners are becoming interested in signing her for their films, even before her first film is out. Because, she already has a huge youthful following on social media which is sure to be a ready audience for her films."

"Yes, and I am the one that both my family and the audience have long forgotten," Aryaa said as tears started streaming down her face.

Vijay paused for a moment, letting Aryaa vent all her bottled emotions and insecurities before making a quiet suggestion.

Aryaa listened to Vijay's idea intently and then said, "Oh Vijay, do you think this will work? What if…"

"Don't worry your pretty head over it. Just focus on playing your hand smartly," Vijay said, soothing his former love and longstanding friend.

*

Later that week, K.K. Bedi thoughtfully organized a family dinner, for all members to meet and reconcile before the big announcements. He knew there was a storm brewing. Aryaa and Prerna had the daggers out for each other, and he wanted to get that confrontation over and done with at a private gathering rather than have a public bust-up in front of the cameras.

Understandably, on the day of the said dinner, he was pacing about nervously, praying that the girls would bury their animosity and come together in support of his business. He must have prayed really hard or earnestly, because the sit-down went off smoothly without any incident. In fact, Aryaa, after being reserved initially, spent almost the entire evening chatting with Prerna.

"Dad, I have been hearing such good things about Prerna in industry circles. I can't wait to watch her in this big film you are announcing," Aryaa finally said cheerfully to him when they caught a moment together.

"Yes, yes of course," K.K. Bedi replied cautiously, relief writ large on his face.

Not one to be left behind in scoring brownie points with their father, Prerna piped up too, "But, Aryaa, you are just amazing. I have to confess that I've only watched just one film of yours – your debut – but you're so good, so glamorous and confident in it."

Prerna, who had been very scared of facing Aryaa, had evidently warmed up to her. As the evening wore on, they were posting photos and comments on their Insta accounts.

The smile on K.K. Bedi's face had widened considerably by now and they posed for a father-daughter selfie, capturing the moment for posterity, setting off a viral storm on Instagram.

When they finally said their goodbyes, the girls seemed to be getting along like a house on fire. In fact, Prerna insisted on dropping Aryaa to her apartment.

I can sleep peacefully tonight. This is an auspicious start to tomorrow's big announcements, K.K. Bedi thought to himself.

*

The venue for the press conference, Grand Intercontinental Hotel, a hotbed of glamorous visitors on any given day, was splashed with banners. Numerous media vans were parked outside and Aryaa looked thrilled. She had missed it – all the attention, the crazy intrusive borderline offensive questions, everything.

She met Prerna and their father at the entrance and the flashbulbs went crazy. To see the two stepsisters, known for sharing rather cold vibes, smiling at each other in one frame, was priceless. The girls knew exactly how to work the crowd of reporters and photographers into a frenzy. The siblings knew that each and every one in the media present was closely observing their action and movements. So, the sisters leaned into each other, adjusting each other's hair, smiling and laughing at their personal jokes in full view of the camera. They posed and then walked self-consciously towards the stage. After the crowd had settled down and the MC had made the introductions, the press was allowed to ask questions.

Vaibhav from *Bollywood Post* piped up and said, "Prerna, we just heard that your next film is going to be with Vijay and obviously there is one you are doing for Bedi Films, so which will it be first?"

K.K. Bedi looked as though somebody had just shot him in the head.

Prerna smiled.

"Nothing escapes you guys, na," chirped Prerna. "Yes, I am doing a film opposite Vijay very soon but let's talk about the Bedi Films project for now. That's the reason why we are here."

Aryaa stayed quiet, waiting her turn. If she knew her father well, he would not let this go. His ego was the biggest thing about him – bigger than his creativity and business acumen put together.

Sure enough, K.K. Bedi recovered from the shock, took the mike, and after a cheerful greeting announced, "Thank you for joining us. The actual reason we are here is to announce my elder daughter Aryaa's comeback film. Not as a director, as you all have been speculating, but as an actor. Yes! Aryaa is the heroine of our next film. It is a very challenging role, about a married woman struggling to resurrect her career. Aryaa is the reason that we could start Bedi Films and I am very sure that with her return, Bedi Films will once again touch the dizzying heights of fame. As for my younger girl, Prerna, she is here to lend her support for the film and yes, there is a cameo that she plays but we can't divulge more than that now – it will kill the surprise. You must watch the film to see both my girls in action!"

Prerna looked stunned. But she was thrown only for a second before she put a charming smile back on her face again.

Aryaa knew it was her turn to shine. She cupped her mouth with her hands, to express her surprise, and then wiping some tears she had marshalled, turned to her father and embraced him in a warm bear hug.

"Oh, Daddy, I'm so grateful! What a surprise, you two," she trilled. Turning back to the audience she continued, "Guys, we had a family dinner last night and neither my father nor my sister gave me even a single clue of what they were plotting and planning!" Aryaa embraced KK and Prerna in a group hug of sorts while planting a kiss on Prerna's cheek.

Truth be told, despite being in on it, Aryaa *was* surprised. She had never in her wildest dream imagined that this big gamble would turn out exactly as planned.

Vijay's prediction had been proved right yet again. Vijay had told her, "I definitely want to work with Prerna, but cannot approach her without your help. So, convince her for me. It's going to be great for both of us."

And the best part of his plan was that K.K. Bedi would never forgive Prerna for working in a film with Vijay. "If I know your father's ego even a little bit, he will immediately cast aside anyone, including Prerna, who goes against his wishes. And you, darling, will most certainly land the heroine's role after all this!"

"And you, my friend, will have a young new star for your next film! You will reconnect with the youth and reinvent yourself for a new generation. I hate to admit it, but Prerna and you will look good together as a couple even though she's almost fifteen years your junior!" Aryaa ribbed her friend.

Aryaa had diligently followed the next part of Vijay's instructions. She casually mentioned Vijay's interest to Prerna over dinner to gauge her reaction. Finding Prerna rather interested, Aryaa had connected Vijay and her younger stepsister on the drive back from dinner, and the deal was sealed over the phone call itself.

Prerna was excited that the biggest superstar in Bollywood, Vijay, was offering her a heroine's role opposite him, and immediately said yes to it. She had been shielded by her mother from old industry gossip and enmities. She hadn't known about Vijay and KK's history. The unsuspecting youngster had no idea that it would cost her big time on the home banner front.

But all was not lost.

Prerna went on to be part of a youthful blockbuster, which basically rode on the shoulders of the male star, Vijay. She then signed on a slew of generic films with big megastars and became what is known as a staple Hindi film heroine.

Aryaa went on to win a National Award with her comeback film under the Bedi banner. Bedi Productions now makes 'meaningful' films suited for a new and aware audience.

Last heard, K.K. Bedi was looking for another good script and new-age director for their undisputed Golden Goose Aryaa's next film as heroine.

Thappad Ki Goonj

Tej Kharbanda, a young twenty-something director had been in the news lately, thanks to his cutting-edge independent film *Siyaahi*, about a young Dalit writer who, using his pen, takes revenge against the upper-class tormentors in his village.

Tej was now being talked about as a truly iconoclastic film-maker who had burst onto the scene and showed enough promise to create cinema which could reach deep into the heart of India. The new Satyajit Ray-meets-Anurag Kashyap.

Today, Tej was seated at the bar area of Bohemian House, the new creative hotspot in Mumbai's Juhu area that had practically everybody vying for one of its limited-edition memberships. It was not uncommon to spot Bollywood bigwigs letting their hair down in its calming seaside precincts where no cameras or cell phones were allowed. Being a Monday afternoon, the bar was mellow for a change. The happening hipster flock of creatives had not yet descended in full force.

Sipping on a beetroot juice that was a beautiful shade of deep crimson, Tej seemed a picture of the chilled-out creative guy. In truth, he was very excited. Thus far in his film-making career, he had struggled very hard, writing screenplays for peanuts then assisting various directors, and so on, to finally get his big break. Now with the success of his debut independent film he had wangled a meeting with a top talent management agency that was keen to sign him on. Tej had just finished the meeting where he had been promised that signing up with the agency would help him break into the big league of Bollywood.

Tej had stayed back after the meeting to savour the moment. Stepping out of the bar he walked into the adjoining balcony that overlooked the Juhu Beach. The impressive sight of the Arabian Sea glistening in the distance brought home the reality that Tej was in Mumbai, the City of Dreams, his own dream on the verge of coming true. He was about to light up and smoke a quick cigarette, when through the French windows of the balcony he noticed a noisy group of plump oldish men dressed in clothes meant for buff youngsters come into the bar. Although they were just four people in the group, they marched to the biggest table near the seaside balcony and pulled up seats and sofas almost blocking off the entire corner area.

The staff stood around watching helplessly. None having the courage to say a word to stop the blatant rearrangement of the furniture.

Tej, still lingering on the balcony, watched the entourage going about their rowdy routine. He chuckled to himself. The old men were a hoot, with their trying-too-hard-to-be-trendy attire. With heavily worked-on faces all of them looked like wax statues of their former selves, their skin pulled so tightly across their faces that even the hint of a smile could rip it apart at the seams.

It was only after a few minutes when Tej heard the raucous bunch loudly applaud someone that it struck him that at the centre of the noisy old men was Raunak Singh, the yesteryears Bollywood star who was famous for his flashy films and flashier lifestyle. Wearing dark glasses and his trademark hat with a cigarette tucked in the corner of his mouth, the now paunchy Raunak Singh was reciting one of his legendary lines from one of his hit films. A line that Tej had heard many times while growing up. Not from watching Raunak Singh's films repeatedly, but recited to him by Tej's own grandfather, his beloved dadaji, Karunesh Kharbanda.

Tej Kharbanda was an outsider in the film industry, a fact that he maintained rather publicly and proudly. But not many knew that Tej's tenuous link with movies went back two generations to his dadaji, who, after an unexpected tryst with Bollywood in the early 1970s, had returned to the fold with a resolve to never look back again.

Karunesh had set up a small business in his home town, Jabalpur, and spawned a small family that grew up together in a modest home in the city. To soften the harsh grind of middle-class existence and to pass the time, Karunesh would often regale his extended family with anecdotes about his time spent with Hindi movie stars of filmi duniya before it became famous as Bollywood. Karunesh's storytelling sessions were always big-ticket events for young Tej and his siblings. They got to hear some mindboggling stories about famous film stars and their shenanigans. These storytelling sessions were also held on popular demand when visiting friends and relatives would insist that Dadaji regale them with the gems from his days in Bombay. Tej in particular always looked forward to these stories. Especially, because his dadaji was always playing a central cameo in all of them.

Of course, like all fables, Dadaji's stories too had a moral. It was an odd coincidence that the moral in all of Dadaji's stories often suggested that no self-respecting person should contemplate a career in the movies. Tej always wondered why. To him Hindi films were a magical, wondrous way to explore creativity. Something that he dreamt about indulging in some day. And then life got in the way. Being the good middle-class small-town boy, Tej was forced to drink the Kool-Aid of 'education-leads-to-a-good-job-which-leads-to-success'. He did put his nose to the educational grindstone but, fate often has a mind of its own. Despite being a bright student who cleared engineering entrance exams with flying colours and went on to become an electronics engineer, Tej rebelliously decided to follow his heart. He quit the rat race before joining it, and enrolled and completed a film-direction and editing course at FTII in Pune and eventually, landed up in Mumbai.

Today, as Tej stood smoking on the Bohemian House balcony feeling on top-of-the-world, he was reminded of the last story that his dadaji had told him just before he died. The real story of his life in Bollywood.

Like several others, Karunesh Kharbanda had landed in Mumbai from Jabalpur to become an actor. He had a reasonably good physique, a pleasant face and he could mimic famous actors delivering their punchiest of dialogues. Back home, Karunesh had become something of a local celebrity, often invited to weddings to regale corpulent film-star obsessed families with his imitations.

At one such gathering, he was advised for the millionth time to try his luck in Bombay, the city of dreams and entertainers.

Another helpful know-it-all suggested he try his hand in theatre which gave opportunity to youngsters like him who had talent but no godfathers.

Karunesh's parents, regular middle-class folks, were both proud and anxious. But, they had packed him off to Bombay with all the money the sale of their assets could muster. In time-honoured tradition, he had initially parked himself at a relative's house to find his feet in the megalopolis that was Bombay. Karunesh's optimism knew no bounds. After learning of the hotspots – hanging at the various drama theatres, at Juhu Beach, at film shoots – he joined the regular stream of acting aspirants who went knocking from one film producer's door to another until all possible doors had been knocked upon. Unfortunately, doors just wouldn't open for him even though he tried hard. He soon attained the hoary status of being a 'struggler'. But, instead of losing heart he become even more determined to continue with the struggle.

Unlike many young hopefuls of those times, Karunesh was a fitness freak with an excellent athletic physique. Juhu Beach was a place he often used for his fitness schedule. Running, skipping, somersaults, karate – you name it and Karunesh was in the process of mastering it.

One morning at the beach, he was engrossed in performing his somersaulting stunts. So deep was his concentration that he did not realize that a crowd had gathered near him. When he snapped out of his trance, Karunesh suddenly became aware of the crowd and for a moment thought that it had gathered for him. Then to his utter surprise, he realized that among the crowd was film star Raunak Singh who had been standing there watching Karunesh's antics with his gang of morning-walk friends.

"What you do is fantastic. Superb. What's your name?" asked Raunak Singh.

Before the star-struck Karunesh could reply, Raunak Singh imperiously said, "Come and meet me. The industry needs people like you." And off went Raunak Singh with his entourage towards his posh seaside bungalow at the end of the beach. If Karunesh had ever harboured any thoughts of going back home, they vanished that very instant.

With great agency, a few days later, Karunesh figured out where he could get to meet Raunak Singh and landed up on the sets of the star's new film. He spotted one of Raunak's beach-entourage members hanging around the set. He casually enquired from unit hands and got the information that the man he had spotted was Peony Bhai, Raunak's 'right-hand'. So, Karunesh walked up to the point till which bystanders were allowed, and called out to Peony Bhai, reminding him of the beach encounter. Peony Bhai ignored Karunesh. He was after all a watchful gatekeeper to his lord and master, Raunak Singh, whose time, he was certain, should not be spent on wastrels.

In a desperate attempt to catch Peony Bhai's attention, Karunesh broke into a somersault right then and there. In a moment that could only be described as miraculous, Raunak Singh appeared almost magically at the studio entrance and spotted Karunesh performing his stunts in a bid to impress Peony Bhai. He snapped his fingers like a maharaja and Peony Bhai went running to him with his cigarettes and lighter. A spot boy ran over with a folding chair. Raunak strode across and sat on a chair.

"Ah, the *beachwala* stuntman! Why don't you perform again for me?" he said jovially.

Karunesh was only too happy to oblige. He did a double-somersault this time. Finishing with a flourish he landed straight at Raunak Singh's feet.

"Sir, just give me an opportunity, I will do anything," Karunesh pleaded with Raunak.

Raunak Singh smiled and said, "Hmmm. *Theek hai*, Mr *Kartab Baaz*. Wait here." He called the director of the film to join them and asked Karunesh to repeat his stunts.

Karunesh happily obliged again.

"*Chalega*?" Raunak Singh turned to the director and asked.

"He is a little shorter and thinner than you, but he's good, so if we keep him in long shots and back to camera and cheat, we should be able to manage," the director said, his eyebrows knitting furiously as he tried to envisage the scene.

"Okay then, you get started today," said Raunak Singh to Karunesh. With that he stood up abruptly, got into a swanky car and left.

Karunesh's joy knew no bounds. He called his parents, telling them happily that he was about to step in as a body-double for hero Raunak Singh, the biggest action star of the time. He was in luck that Raunak Singh had had a severe back injury recently and had not completely recovered from it.

"*Mata rani ki kripa hai*," his mother said to him.

And thus began an unlikely association with Raunak Singh.

Each day Karunesh would land up at the film sets and wait to be called for some shot or the other. But each day, he would be left unused and disappointed. Each day he would be told that he would be needed the next day. The silver lining in the cloud was that each day he received fifty rupees for his presence on the set. He would go back home, buy himself some food and sometimes a quarter bottle of rum and gulp it down, thanking his stars that at least he was in the system. Each night he would sleep hoping that the next day his moment would arrive.

Despite this, Karunesh believed that his dreams had nearly come true and he was ever grateful to Raunak Singh for making it happen. Some nights, Karunesh was allowed to join in the post-shooting drinking sessions that Raunak Singh and his friends had on the sets. Karunesh's job was to fix the drinks for Raunak and his closest friends whenever he saw their glasses near empty. In fact, Karunesh realised that Raunak Singh began to rely on his ability to fix just the right measure of whiskey and soda that he liked. Raunak Singh would regularly heap praise on him as an expert drink-fixer. Karunesh would feel chuffed every time he was praised. In Karunesh's mind Raunak Singh soon achieved a godlike status.

"I can do anything for sir," he confessed his fervent devotion to Peony Bhai while clearing up after one such night of heavy drinking by Raunak Singh and his entourage.

"Anything?" Peony Bhai shot back with a wink.

"Anything. Anything done for God is good," Karunesh trilled with all the earnestness of a devotee.

Peony Bhai sat quietly for a minute and then said, "I will keep that in mind and also tell Raunak sir. But you had better remember it when the time comes."

Karunesh didn't quite get the drift, but he was too happy to really care.

The time arrived soon after, while shooting for a film at a massive village set constructed in Film City. Karunesh was summoned urgently by Peony Bhai to go and see Raunak in the makeshift private tent that had been set up for the star.

Karunesh's heart leaped with excitement as he entered Raunak Singh's tent. Inside, it was dark with just a dim kerosene lamp on the table making eerie shadows leap up and down on the walls. Raunak was sitting on a folding chair that had been set up for him in the darkest corner of the tent. His shoulders and his posture were slumped and Karunesh could barely recognize his face in the darkness.

"Raunak sir?" Karunesh ventured.

No response. Just the stench of alcohol.

"Raunak sir?"

This time, he was answered by the smashing of a glass. Before Karunesh could gather his wits, Raunak stood up suddenly and towered over him. He raised his right hand and without warning started slapping Karunesh repeatedly across his face. Karunesh was too shocked to cry out. He just stood still while Raunak slapped him with all his might across both his cheeks. The blows stung hard and tears welled up in Karunesh's eyes. A few seconds later Karunesh recovered enough to ask, "Sir … Sir, what's the matter? Have I done something wrong?"

By now Raunak seemed tired. All his energy spent, he sat down and slumped back again in his chair, signalling Karunesh away wordlessly with a brusque wave of the hand.

Karunesh staggered out, looking devastated. Even in his confusion he knew that he had to speak to Peony Bhai immediately. Peony Bhai was waiting for him right outside. He took Karunesh aside, and to his surprise, gave him a sympathetic hug. Before Karunesh could say anything, Peony Bhai spoke in an extremely placatory tone, "Don't worry about what just happened. When he gets very angry about something, it is necessary to get someone on whom he can vent his anger. Raunak sir will keep getting you work as extra or junior artiste or body-double and in return every once in a way you have to tolerate his *gussa*."

Karunesh could only manage to say, "But, but…"

Peony Bhai cut in before he could finish his sentence. "What difference does it make to you. You are sturdy enough. And you said that he is your God and you could do anything for God. Look at this as his *prasad*."

Karunesh fell silent, not knowing what to say and how to respond.

Peony Bhai then checked Karunesh for any injuries, and finding none, summarily packed him off.

Karunesh was in a daze when he reached his room that he was now sharing with other strugglers. His relatives had politely refused to extend Karunesh's stay after three months of free boarding and lodging, and of course the discovery of some of Karunesh's harmless flirting with the neighbour's daughter hadn't helped.

As he lay in bed, he tossed and turned thinking about the incident. Somewhere in the wee hours of the morning he came to a conclusion. If this is what his God was giving him, he must ask for some suitable reward for this penance.

The next day, Karunesh was still smarting. Not so much from the physical blows as from the shock and humiliation of the task he had been entrusted with. But Peony Bhai tried to apply a monetary salve on his bruised ego and handed him a reasonable sum of money to compensate for the incident with a promise that this would lead to more substantial work.

Days passed. The months went by. Karunesh discovered that real good work did not come his way except as an extra in some scenes. But the *thappads* from Raunak Singh came at regulars bouts. Fortunately, so did the post-beating money, letting him stretch his Bombay dreams a little more.

Unfortunately, the news about Karunesh's real job leaked out and soon the film hands had a nickname for Karunesh. *Thappadwala*. When he came to know of his moniker, Karunesh's self-respect took a nosedive. The cheerful, ever-optimistic Karunesh developed a nervous tic and his smile shrunk to a tight thin line on his face.

One day he spotted Raunak Singh with just Peony Bhai at the studio make-up room and went to him with folded hands almost begging for better work. "Raunak sir, you are very kind but please give me some real work now. I came here to be a part of the movies as an actor not just an extra."

Raunak Singh looked at him, and with scathing disdain said, "Even monkeys can jump and do stunts, but the difference between them and you is that they know they are not actors. They are happy doing what they can do. You, on the other hand have become delusional because of my kindness."

Karunesh recoiled in horror as though Raunak Singh had struck him again physically with one of his muscled hands. His face crumpled and tears streamed down his face. He stepped away quietly. Peony Bhai looked guilty and shuffled his feet, watching Karunesh walk away.

The next day, Karunesh came on the set quietly to Raunak Singh's tent and handed over a big bouquet and a bottle of what seemed to be choicest whiskey.

"Sir, I am leaving town. What you told me about monkeys was very helpful in making up my mind."

Raunak Singh didn't bat an eye and waved him away with a flippant wave of the hand.

Aware of Raunak Singh's ways – he would drink on the set and then take the party to Sunny Sands with his entourage and drink again like a fish – Karunesh just bowed in a servile manner, his hands folded in a gesture of deference.

"Sir, have a peg before I leave, I will feel happy to have returned your favour," he said.

Raunak Singh did not need much persuasion. Glasses were called for. But Karunesh's offering, despite being a premium label, was not up to Raunak Singh's high standards. "Where did you get the whiskey from, you oaf?" asked Raunak as he took another gulp to check. He made a face and then kept his glass aside and went for his shot. "Cheap bloody duplicate booze from a cheap *ganwaar,*" he spat out.

Karunesh left Bombay that day never to return again.

Back in Jabalpur, Karunesh bid goodbye to all his filmi fancies and used his meagre savings to set up a small grocery shop. He got married. Soon, he had a son and a daughter, and worked from morning to night with his nose buried in the shop's account book.

He died at the age of sixty-five with no debts and an extended happy family that truly mourned his passing. Karunesh never told anyone, except his grandson Tej, about the ignominy he had endured during his stint in the film industry.

Tej took a deep drag on his cigarette, remembering his dadaji's last moments. Then stubbed it out and stepped off the balcony of Bohemian House and re-entered the bar.

He casually walked up to Raunak Singh's table, smiled and said, "Raunak sir, let your drinks be on me today. I've just made a hit film and I'm celebrating. And then I am also a big fan. I need your blessings too."

Tej signalled to the waiter.

Raunak Singh looked up from the table, the film star within him instantly alert and preening.

"*Shukriya, dost*. It's thanks to people like you that Raunak Singh is still legend. What's your name?"

"Tej Kharbanda, I'm the writer-director of *Siyaahi*."

"Oh! Achha … haan …Wonderful film."

The waiter arrived with stiff pegs of the choicest Scotch whiskey for everyone at the table. Tej poured the drinks.

"Cheers, young director," said everyone, raising their glasses.

"*Shukriya*," said Tej. "By the way, Raunak sir, my grandfather worked for you years ago. I am Karunesh Kharbanda's grandson."

Raunak Singh's expression changed instantly. Tej could sense some hostility. He tried to say something but Raunak Singh interrupted.

"So now the descendants of junior artistes have started becoming award-winning directors! The world sure has changed!"

The entourage of old-fogeys tittered at Raunak Singh's attempt at humour.

Tej was silent.

Then Raunak Singh spoke again. "*Chalo*, god bless. But don't run away from Bombay like your grandfather … don't be afraid of hard work," he said with a malicious smile.

The men guffawed.

Tej took a deep breath as he had learnt in his meditation class. He now understood the humiliation his grandfather had faced and in that moment, knew he had to avenge him. And he knew exactly what to do. But, Tej was a creative guy and not someone given to violent outbursts. Calm personified, he said, "Yes, sir, absolutely. You are right. I will stay put here. But if you allow, let me complete the task that Dadaji couldn't finish."

Raunak Singh was now getting impatient. "What task?" he asked, irritated.

"You remember … that last bottle of whiskey my grandfather brought you before leaving Bombay? That last peg he served you? Well, he made that peg in the bathroom assigned to junior artistes … in the urinal. You did say something about the way it tasted, didn't you? Do you remember the taste?"

A deathly silence fell over the group. Raunak Singh's smile froze on his face.

It was Tej's turn to smile, "Arrey! Don't worry, sir. This time *maine jo drink aap ke liye banayi hai* that has come straight from the bar … no adulteration. Have a sip and tell me what you think."

Raunak Singh dropped the glass of whiskey he was holding to the ground!

An old paunchy fellow, who fit the description of Peony Bhai, turned and threw up on the side of the table.

Tej, calm as a cucumber, folded his hands in a namaste and left the bar.

Getting into the lift, he could not stop laughing out loud. He had followed Dadaji's advice – the best revenge is to let the imagination of your enemy do your work for you! And, it certainly had. Now this would definitely be a Bollywood story that his dadaji would love to listen to.

Acknowledgements

Every book is a labour of love for an author, so it is for me. However, *Folktales from Bollywood* is special because it marks my leap into the world of fiction.

The idea for the book came to me in the thick of pandemic doom. In the midst of the despair, to dispel the sombre mood that prevailed and purely to entertain family and friends over lengthy phone calls, I took to relating pithy anecdotes about Bollywood. Over time, these conversations proved to be a springboard for my imagination.

So, to all the people I spoke to during those dark days, thank you for setting off the spark of light.

To my husband, Piyush, I owe a debt of gratitude for my foray into writing fiction. He played mentor, cheerleader and disciplinarian, insisting that I put pen and paper to my flights of fancy and capture the stories that were spinning around in my head.

To my parents, I owe thanks, as always, for their feedback on the stories, and for their good wishes for my new endeavour.

A heartfelt note of gratitude to the inimitable author, columnist and journalist Shobhaa De. An intrepid and fearless opinion-maker, she is someone whom one has long admired and looked up to, for her thought-provoking perspective on things that matter. A big 'Thank You' to her for making time in an impossibly busy schedule to read the book and give her 'verdict'. It is, indeed, a dream come true.

To Kanishka Gupta, my literary agent, a big thank you, for his encouraging words and unfailing faith in my debut work in fiction. This book certainly would not have been possible without him.

A salute to Shantanu Ray Chaudhuri, editor par excellence, who I was fortunate to have on my project. His deep knowledge and sure-handed guidance and sustained patience ensured that the book landed just right. And thank you, Chakrika Pandey, for the fine-toothed comb in going through the text.

And last but not the least, a doff of my hat to my publisher Ajay Mago, the man with the Midas touch, someone who always has the best advice and is both innovative and ever supportive with his counsel on the direction that is best for one's book.